THE
ULTIMATE
COMPETITIVE
ADVANTAGE

THE
ULTIMATE
COMPETITIVE
ADVANTAGE

WHY YOUR PEOPLE MAKE ALL THE DIFFERENCE AND THE 6 PRACTICES YOU NEED TO ENGAGE THEM

SHAWN D. MOON and
SUE DATHE-DOUGLASS

FOREWORD BY SEAN COVEY

A FRANKLINCOVEY BOOK

BenBella Books, Inc.
Dallas, Texas

BenBella Books, Inc.
10300 N. Central Expressway, Suite #530
Dallas, TX 75231
www.benbellabooks.com
Send feedback to feedback@benbellabooks.com

Printed in the United States of America
10 9 8 7 6 5 4 3 2

Library of Congress Cataloging-in-Publication Data
Moon, Shawn D. (Shawn Daniel), 1967-
  The ultimate competitive advantage : why your people make all the difference and the 6 practices you need to engage them / Shawn Moon and Sue Dathe-Douglass ; foreword by Sean Covey.
    pages cm
   ISBN 978-1-940363-63-9 (hardback) — ISBN 978-1-940363-64-6 (electronic)
1. Leadership. 2. Corporate culture. 3. Organizational behavior. 4. Organizational effectiveness. 5. Employee motivation. I. Title.
  HD57.7.M6387 2015
  658.3'14—dc23

                                                            2014026426

Editing by Debbie Harmsen
Copyediting by James Fraleigh
Proofreading by Jenny Bridges and Harrison Flanders
Indexing by Clive Pyne Book Indexing Services
Cover design by Bradford Foltz
Jacket design by Sarah Dombrowsky
Text design by Silver Feather Design
Text composition by PerfecType, Nashville, TN
Printed by Lake Book Manufacturing

Distributed by Perseus Distribution
(www.perseusdistribution.com)

To place orders through Perseus Distribution:
Tel: (800) 343-4499 / Fax: (800) 351-5073
E-mail: orderentry@perseusbooks.com

Significant discounts for bulk sales are available. Please contact Glenn Yeffeth at glenn@benbellabooks.com or (214) 750-3628.

CONTENTS

Dedicated to YOU and to all those who seek
the ultimate competitive advantage.

FOREWORD

YOU CAN HAVE THE BEST technology, the most innovative marketing campaign, or the latest product that goes viral—and it can all disappear overnight like dying fireworks. It can all be copied by another competitor or become instantly obsolete in the wake of something new and better.

In this world, all business success is interim. If you're a leader, the only competitive advantage you have is that combination of hearts and brains—yours and your people's—that can produce success again and again. The only assets you can depend on are human beings. The air they live on is passion, high purpose, and psychological, and when they don't get what they need, neither do you.

The fact is, people now need different things than they used to—particularly young people. They need to be leaders themselves. They need to make things happen. They deeply need to be able to trust.

They don't need a career—they need a mission. A career is a profession; a mission is a cause. A career asks, "What's in it for me?" A mission asks, "How can I make a difference?"

And your job now—your mission—is to ignite that kind of fire in yourself and your team. This book, written by my friends and colleagues, will help you ignite that fire. It's about leaving behind an ash heap of assumptions that used to work but now produce stagnation, and moving on to new paradigms that will spark the passion of your people.

Stephen R. Covey, my father, used to say, "We see the world not as it is, but as we are—as we are conditioned to be." As you read this book, you'll be startled out of your old conditioning by a whole new

---

---

set of possibilities. Instead of just being a leader, you can make *everybody* a leader. Instead of just doing more with less, you can do *infinitely* more with less. Instead of just "creating value" for customers, you can become *the very key* to their success.

There's a lot to do in this book, but I challenge you to read it and start right away to identify at least one of the new practices (what we call the "jobs that you must do now") and then create an action plan to improve your individual and team effectiveness in that area. Really work at it. See for yourself if it doesn't transform your work and your business results. Thinking tools at the end of each chapter will help you.

But there's more. If you take this book as a whole, it will help you install in your head a new "operating system" for effectiveness. An operating system is the software that makes your smartphone or laptop work. Most businesspeople have a terribly outdated mental operating system, so they lose efficiency, slow down, and—eventually—totally freeze up.

What you need is an operating system that never goes out of date, that you can rely on forever.

The operating system in this book is based on fundamental principles that are timeless and universal—principles such as proactivity, integrity, trustworthiness, empathy, and valuing diversity. These principles are embedded in my father's bestselling book, *The 7 Habits of Highly Effective People*. If you build on these principles, if you make them the unbreakable foundation of your life's work, your success as a leader is guaranteed no matter what happens.

Is your culture working for you or against you? The actions you take today will prepare you to lead yourself, others, your team, and your organization effectively.

—SEAN COVEY
Author of the international bestseller *The 7 Habits of Highly Effective Teens* and coauthor of the #1 *Wall Street Journal* Business bestseller *The 4 Disciplines of Execution*

CHAPTER 1

A New Paradigm: In a Winning Culture, Everyone Leads

"If you don't have a competitive advantage, don't compete."
—Jack Welch

O UTSIDE THE WORLD OF WOMEN'S collegiate soccer, Coach Anson Dorrance may not be a household name. But anyone who has even the slightest appreciation for women's soccer—or any high-level soccer league for that matter—knows Coach Dorrance of the University of North Carolina (UNC) as a fierce competitor who has created a remarkable culture of winning. The seven-time National Coach of the Year not only has become one of the greatest collegiate soccer coaches of all time, he is also recognized as simply one of the greatest coaches ever in any sport. Period. At one point, his teams achieved a 103-game unbeaten streak. As of this writing, his teams have earned a .935 winning percentage, and thirteen different women he has coached have won a total of twenty

National Player of the Year awards. And this individual achievement has translated to team achievement, as UNC's women's soccer teams have won twenty-one national championships (and counting). When legendary UNC men's basketball coach Dean Smith was asked about Carolina's preseason number one ranking in football and what it was like for a sport other than basketball to be ranked number one, he replied, "This is a women's soccer school. We're just trying to keep up with them."[1]

Coach Dorrance creates the framework for engagement and synergy, and the athletes integrate their individual contributions into that framework. His athletes understand their respective roles. They take ownership of their individual part of the team and weave it into the overall team scheme. They quickly realize the level of commitment required for Coach Dorrance's system, and they work daily to live up to that commitment.

Coach Dorrance clearly attracts extraordinary talent to his program. There is a legacy of winning, a culture of peak performance that acts as a magnet for top talent. But most collegiate athletic programs have amazing talent. Great short- and long-term results require more than that. They require leadership at every level. They require a common language. They require all stakeholders to have clarity around goals and top priorities. They require a system for accomplishing these goals. They require trust and loyalty among (and beyond) the team. In short, they require a winning culture. That is what Coach Dorrance has established. His results are not simply one and done. He has sustained them for more than thirty years.

> "People talk about being part of something larger than themselves, of being connected, of being generative."
> —PETER M. SENGE

While this example highlights the importance of a winning culture under a highly effective leader, the sports arena is certainly not the only place this applies. This same type of culture, where people get excited about you and your product, can happen in the department or organization you're leading, too. You can raise your team from ordinary, good, or even great to extraordinary by focusing on how to get all team members to take ownership of their roles.

Think about what it feels like to be part of a winning team, one that achieves success again and again. You might have experienced this on the athletic fields or courts. Perhaps it was with a musical group or academic team, or even on a work assignment. Think about how engaged you felt, about your level of accountability, about how you acted toward your teammates or colleagues, about the results you achieved. MIT lecturer Peter M. Senge makes this observation about that experience in his book *The Fifth Discipline*:

> When you ask people about what it is like being part of a great team, what is most striking is the meaningfulness of the experience. People talk about being part of something larger than themselves, of being connected, of being generative. It becomes quite clear that, for many, their experiences as part of truly great teams stand out as singular periods of life lived to the fullest. Some spend the rest of their lives looking for ways to recapture that spirit.[2]

After thirty years of partnering with some of the greatest organizations and leaders worldwide, we know that there are a handful of things that make them remarkable. Think of top-notch organizations you know—ones you would (and do) recommend wholeheartedly to others, sometimes passionately. Why? What makes them so unique? What causes you to feel so strongly about these organizations? In our experience, they share the most powerful, hard-to-replicate, and sustainable competitive advantage—a winning culture.

WHAT IS CULTURE?

Many definitions of culture have been advanced throughout the years, but for our purposes we will define it as the collective behavior of your people (what the majority of your people do the majority of the time); the nature of the language and relationships within the organization; and the spoken and unspoken values, norms, and systems at work therein. Winning cultures are filled with superb people who deliver as promised time after time.

Winning cultures are unique, deliberately designed and maintained, and rare.

They give you someone and something to trust. Winning cultures are unique, deliberately designed and maintained, and rare.

A CULTURE EXPOSED WITH THE RISING TIDE

Let's visit a culture we have been privileged to work with over the past seven years: Western Digital. Our work with Western Digital (WD) began with FranklinCovey training the WD leadership team in the principles of our book *The 7 Habits of Highly Effective People*. Porntip Iyimapun, our FranklinCovey partner in Thailand, met with the leadership at WD and identified that the company's purpose in bringing us in was to create a culture with principles as the core operating system. This initial work with WD's leadership team was

CULTURE: *the collective behavior of your people (what the majority of your people do the majority of the time); the nature of the language and relationships within the organization; and the spoken and unspoken values, norms, and systems at work therein.*

followed by years of additional training by internal facilitators and champions, targeted at all levels of the organization.

Just as an individual's character is tested the most when it is under pressure, an organization's culture is exposed during times of crisis. The culture at Western Digital was tested one humid summer and early fall.

The 2011 rainy season in Thailand was the heaviest in fifty years. The flooding started in July in the north, and within two months the highly populated southern region around Bangkok was underwater, with near panic as people struggled to find high ground. Thirteen million were displaced and more than eight hundred died. It was called the fourth most expensive disaster in history.

Sue was working in Bangkok as the devastating flood approached. As she describes it, "It was so strange and unnerving to experience this always-bustling city in a ghostlike, eerily quiet, suspended state. Every day the sandbags around my hotel rose higher and higher until they were at least eight feet high. People were parking their cars on elevated expressways hoping to save them from the inevitable washing away of familiar streets and alleyways. It felt like a very bad version of the Chicken Little nursery rhyme—you knew the flood was coming, you just didn't know when or where. The day-after-day foreboding was unbearable, as was the deep and profound sense of doom."

> Just as an individual's character is tested the most when it is under pressure, an organization's culture is exposed during times of crisis.

By October 15, the flood had driven hundreds of thousands of workers out of the massive Bang Pa-In Industrial Park, a high-tech manufacturing center north of Bangkok. WD's hard-disk manufacturing facility went under nearly six feet of water, devastating an operation that requires a zero-dust environment because a single speck of dirt can destroy a product. It was a calamity.

When it was all over, experts estimated that it would take a billion dollars and at least seven months of cleanup to get even part of the WD factory back on line, while much of the high-end equipment would require years to replace. Some market reports even predicted the end of the company, which would leave nearly 35,000 workers without jobs. The effects were immediate and global, as high-tech manufacturing everywhere ground to a halt without the key components from Thailand. It was called "the monsoon felt around the world."

But Western Digital's leaders didn't want to take years to get back to work, so they took things into their own hands. They immediately spread the word that there would be no layoffs—they were a team and they were going to get on their feet together. The safety of their people came first; crews were organized to help the most stricken employees and their homes. On day two, they hired Thai navy crews to salvage irreplaceable equipment and get it to dry land for refurbishing.

Meanwhile, the plants of other big companies in the industrial park, with their workers laid off, lay rusting and drowning in mud. Six months after the flood, 284 factories remained closed and nearly 165,000 people were still out of work. One observer wrote, "Workers clad in ghost white stood around shuttered factories, like the idle employees of a suspended space program."[3]

But at Western Digital, the work went on nonstop. The fact that everyone remained on payroll certainly made a difference, but rebuilding the business themselves came naturally to these remarkable workers. Tens of thousands, many still trying to cope with the crisis at their homes, showed up to revive their plant. Some traveled miles each day from refugee centers, often in small boats or on water oxen for hours a day, determined to show up for work.

Many found themselves doing jobs they had never done before— hard, muddy manual labor. Company leaders rolled up their sleeves and labored alongside office workers used to the comfort of a desk job. Workers who had never met before formed teams and solved problems on the spot.

The result? On November 30, only forty-six days from its closing, only fifteen days after the waters receded, Western Digital reopened the plant, and within a year it reclaimed the number one position in the market. The firm remained profitable through everything, and even managed to acquire one of its top competitors. Observers were astonished that it hadn't taken billions of dollars and many years to recover. All it took was a superb team willing to wade through mud for each other. (A video clip at www.franklincovey.com/uca will introduce you to the Western Digital culture as the company navigated the 2011 flood.)

A CULTURE THAT SINKS WITH BAD LEADERSHIP

Let's look at a different story of culture and the behaviors, language, and results it produces.

Jan and her sister were in the garden enjoying a cup of coffee, when her sister's husband, Tom, joined them. As he sat down, he glanced at his smartphone: "One year, three months, two days, six hours, four minutes, and . . . exactly thirty seconds until I retire!"

"What are you talking about?" Jan asked. Tom was bright and able and had years of great work ahead of him, or so she thought.

"I've got an app on my phone that counts down to the moment I retire."

Jan knew this must be a joke. "You're not going to retire, Tom. With your background, your company will hire you back as a consultant—and pay you five times as much."

"No," Tom responded. "You don't get it. At the last second on the countdown I can retire with all my benefits, and I'm not working for that company one second past that."

"Why not?"

"My company used to be a great place to work," he said. "I loved everything about it, but two years ago things really changed. We got a new boss, and he came down and told us how things were going to be from now on. Some of us had been around for a few years, so we asked, 'Do we have any say in all this?' I also remarked, 'We have appreciated the loyalty we have felt from the company over the years. Should we continue to expect that?' And he gave us this look . . . well, let's just say it's a look I've gotten familiar with. The new boss then said, rather curtly, 'If you want loyalty, go get a dog.' "

Now, what is Tom's true retirement date? Despite what his smartphone says, he "retired" two years ago. That is when he stopped giving his best to his work, when he ceased being fully engaged. He's been physically on the job, he does what's expected, but nothing more. Tom could have given fifteen or twenty more years—perhaps his finest years—but the firm that used to have his body, mind, spirit, and passion will not benefit from that contribution.

He will give his best to something else.

Could there be a stronger contrast in cultures between the ineffective company that Tom has "retired" from and the highly effective team at Western Digital?

THE CHALLENGE OF HUMAN CAPITAL

Just under a century ago, top business leaders in North America formed an organization called the Conference Board. Its purpose was to get at the truth about what makes business work, and it's still going strong. A scientific enterprise, it's a quiet place that collects data and dispassionately crunches it in an effort to find out what's really going on with the economy.

For many years, the Conference Board has surveyed prominent business leaders across the globe to identify their most critical challenge. Its most recent answer might surprise you:

"Human capital."

What does that mean? *Human* capital? Don't they mean *financial* capital? Why are they worried about human capital? Why is that a top-of-mind issue?

In today's world, with all its attendant challenges, moving pieces, and barrage of information, the key factor between the organizations that will sustain success and those that don't will be the ability to engage one's people to bring their very best. It is the ultimate competitive advantage.

From our experience, gained from the thousands of organizations that have engaged us to help them achieve results where behavioral change is required, we have found that leaders across the globe agree that engaging their talent is their top priority now. They know about the dramatic difference between a Western Digital team and the world of a person like Tom—and how that difference matters more than anything. The ultimate competitive advantage belongs to organizations that can get the best contribution possible from the best people they can find. In simple terms, it means inspiring and motivating people to bring the best they can give—to the point where they will wade through mud for each other!

It begs the question—why is there no "outbreak" of great cultures if so many are aware of both the problem and the opportunity?

Let's explore one of the problems: *The majority of working people are unengaged or actively disengaged from their work.* According to the Gallup Organization, it's 70 percent, and if you factor out leaders and managers, the number approaches 80 percent.[4] That means leaders have failed to motivate and inspire nearly eight out of ten of their workers.

> The majority of working people are unengaged or actively disengaged from their work.

We're talking about literally tens of millions of people like Tom—each one unique, one of a kind, with talent and skill and passion and great contributions to make—who are mentally and emotionally retired.

When Stephen R. Covey spoke to huge audiences around the globe, he would always ask, "How many of you honestly believe that the vast majority of the people in your organization possess more intelligence, talent, capability, creativity, and resourcefulness than their present jobs require or even allow?" In every case, nearly every hand went up.

> "How many of you honestly believe that the vast majority of the people in your organization possess more intelligence, talent, capability, creativity, and resourcefulness than their present jobs require or even allow?"
> —STEPHEN R. COVEY

Why is this so? Because too many business leaders don't know how to engage people. They don't understand that their job is to establish a framework (or operating system, which we'll discuss in Chapter 2) that allows people to contribute their very best—consistently and compellingly. According to the survey on global CEO performance by Stanford University's Center for Leadership Development and Research, engaging people is rated the "top weakness" of CEOs. Some leaders, like Tom's boss, actively discourage people, but most simply don't have the skill to lead people. After reviewing the Stanford study, *Forbes Magazine* concluded that "CEOs are doing a lousy job when it comes to people management."[5]

Leaders know they're not doing a good job managing their people, and it troubles them. They need to know that the job they now must do is to capture the hearts and minds of their people—to build a team like the one at Western Digital. It's the biggest job they have, but they don't know how to do it. And it's not just the CEO's problem; leaders at all levels struggle with it, particularly those who are new in their supervisory roles.

A client of ours, a top leader of a Shanghai engineering firm, opened up to us: "When I graduated from law school, I came out with the very best academic, analytical, research, and legal tools. But what I was not trained on, and what I was not prepared for on day one, was how to coach and engage my people. My first day on the job I had a boss, I had direct reports, I had peers I needed to work with; but I had absolutely no training on how to inspire them or help them to improve performance. Everything I do has to be done with other people. I have to achieve goals with other people. Everything depends on what I was never taught to do."

What this client described is the reason there hasn't been an outbreak of winning cultures. While culture makes all the difference, too many companies leave building their culture to chance. In speaking with thousands of leaders on this subject, we were reminded of a quote by acclaimed management expert Peter Drucker: "Culture eats strategy for breakfast, and it's only when you fully understand what this means that you'll lead a successful company."

THE PEOPLE BEHIND THE ACTIVITIES

You and your people are your organization's only sustainable competitive advantage. No matter what business you're in, when the people quit work for the night, your competitive advantage quits, too. And the brains of a contributor like Tom can shut down any time, even in daylight. "But," you say, "what about my brand? My secret formula? My cost structure? My international partnerships? My Super Bowl commercial? Aren't they competitive advantages?"

Obviously, competitive advantages can come from many sources, but none of those advantages exist apart from what people actually *do*. Your brand, your formula, your cost structure—whatever your resources and capabilities—are all the product of people working together. If *they* don't work well, your advantage is gone.

In his monumental work, *Competitive Advantage*, Michael Porter reasons it out this way: "Is a firm a collection of activities or a set of resources and capabilities? Clearly, a firm is both. But *activities* are what firms do, and they define the resources and capabilities that are relevant . . . Activities are observable, operational, and directly connected to cost and differentiation."[6] In other words, your competitive advantage comes from *activities,* and activities are the things *people* do.

A firm can have a unique brand, but if people don't do the things needed to leverage it, sustain it, and live up to it, it will evaporate. A firm can have an enviable cost structure, but if your people couldn't care less about maintaining it, the whole thing is a house of cards. *The behavior of people is the ultimate source of your competitive advantage.*

No matter what you think your competitive advantage is, *people* create it, sustain it, leverage it, and make it work. If they are as engaged as the people of Western Digital, they will pull the company out of the mud if they have to. But if they are like Tom—unexcited about the company, uncaring, indifferent, even alienated from it—your competitive advantage will disappear. If they are not giving their best efforts to your strategy, you can forget about differentiating yourself in the marketplace. If there are enough Toms in your firm—and the evidence shows there are many Toms, despite what you may think and no matter how often they smile at you as you pass—your competitive advantage is over. As Porter says, "Seeing the firm as a collection of activities makes it clear that *everyone* in a firm is part of strategy."[7]

The sum of what everyone does every day is called "culture," what the majority of the people do the majority of the time. It's a reflection of a company's collective behaviors, the language and behaviors of its people, and the spoken and unspoken values, norms, and systems that exist.

> "Seeing the firm as a collection of activities makes it clear that *everyone* in a firm is part of strategy."
> —MICHAEL PORTER

According to Harvard professor Clayton Christensen, "It is common to describe culture as the visible elements of a working environment: casual Fridays, free sodas in the cafeteria, or whether you can bring your dog to the office . . . Those things don't define a culture. They're just artifacts of it."[8] Culture is much deeper: It's the habitual, instinctive behaviors of people that make up a culture. And those behaviors go even deeper than that: They are rooted in people's character.

Culture is the reason a Western Digital worker wades through flood waters to get the job done. Culture is the reason a Honda line worker stops the workflow if she spots a quality problem. Culture is the reason top-rated Southwest Airlines ground crews run to meet an arriving plane. Culture is the reason why, if your purchase gets stolen from your doorstep, Amazon sends you another one—immediately and at no cost.[9]

But culture is also the reason a great potential contributor like Tom comes to work every day, smiles and nods, and contributes nothing.

Stephen R. Covey once said, "A high-trust culture is the only sustainable competitive advantage." More will be said about how to establish a high-trust culture in Chapter 6, but the behaviors we have mentioned at Western Digital, Honda, Southwest, and Amazon are the behaviors of highly engaged people in a high-trust culture: It's just what they do.

> "If you want to change your culture, change the collective behavior of your leaders."
> —RAM CHARAN

And that kind of culture doesn't just happen. A leader's main job is to build that kind of culture—and to model it, because the behavior of the leader determines the culture. As author Ram Charan said to us once, "The culture of any organization is simply the collective behavior of its leaders. If you want to change your culture, change the collective behavior of your leaders."

CHANGING PARADIGMS

To gain the only sustainable competitive advantage that counts—a great culture—you need to go deep. Human behavior is the product of human character and mindset. It's the product of *paradigms*—the ways people see themselves and the world around them. To change the culture, you have to change people's paradigms.

Shawn tells this simple example of what we mean by a paradigm that drives behavior: "When my wife and I were newly married, we shared one car. She would drop me off at school in the morning before going to her job several miles in the other direction. Then she would drive back at noon to take me to my afternoon job and return to hers. At the end of the day she would circle back and we went home together. We put a lot of miles on our car that semester.

> To change the culture, you have to change people's paradigms.

"One day I needed to be at school early and had a lot of pressing projects at work in the afternoon, so we went carefully over the schedule that morning. She agreed to be prompt picking me up at lunch. So I walked confidently to meet her in the parking area at noon—my wife was nowhere in sight. Forced to wait, I got exponentially more impatient as the minutes passed. This was before mobile phones, and I had no way of contacting her. After about an hour and fifteen minutes, she arrived and explained that she'd had to handle a crisis at work. I was left to swallow my frustration and deal with it.

"Because of the time lost that day, the next day's schedule was especially tight and even fuller than the day before. I now had no margin for error, so when I stepped into the parking lot I knew she'd be there this time. She wasn't—and my temperature rose. I waited and waited and waited. I worried that maybe something had happened to her. Another crisis at work? But after an hour, I determined that if nothing *had* happened, something *would* happen once she finally showed up!

"Then, after two hours and fifteen minutes of pacing and fretting and fuming—a stunning insight! *I had driven the car myself that day!* My wife was waiting for *me*! I gulped hard, trying to think of something to say to her.

"We both chuckle about it now. The point is, I had perceived the situation in a way that didn't fit with reality; and when my paradigm suddenly shifted, my behavior shifted, too. I went from fuming and snarling to groveling and whimpering. That's the power of a paradigm shift."

Sue remembers when she was promoted to head the department where she had been working: "I was delighted, and my many former peers now reporting directly to me seemed delighted, too, that one of their own had been recognized. Nervous and eager to prove myself in my new role, I operated from a paradigm of control, asking that all decisions be run by me as we became comfortable with our new roles. The truth was, I really wanted all of my direct reports to do things *exactly* as I had done—after all, that's what got me promoted. From their perspective, I went from understanding comrade to micromanaging control freak. They just stopped contributing. At times I felt as though they had stopped thinking, and that I needed to be at every meeting injecting energy into every conversation. It took months before I realized it was my paradigm that was creating bottlenecks everywhere. I had slowed down production, disengaged bright and competent leaders, and results were suffering."

Paradigms drive practices. For example, if you're part of a culture that believes in cutthroat competition, you'll probably do anything to bring down your competitors. If, like Sue, you manage within a culture of micromanagement, you'll stifle people and suffocate their potential. In the end, a paradigm based on a false principle will fail you. Your practices or behaviors will bring *you* down.

> [A] paradigm based on a false principle will fail you.

Clayton Christensen says, "A culture can be built consciously or evolve inadvertently."[10] Which do you prefer for your team or workgroup or organization? You can consciously build a culture like Western Digital, or you can let it evolve into a disengaged team of Toms.

CHAPTER 2

THE FRAMEWORK: THE OPERATING SYSTEM THAT BUILDS EFFECTIVE LEADERS AT EVERY LEVEL

"In the Industrial Age, leadership was a position. In the Knowledge Age, leadership is a choice."

—STEPHEN R. COVEY

THROUGHOUT THIS BOOK, WE INVITE you to adopt a new leadership operating system and to "download" the paradigm shifts to your own mind. In doing so, you will discover the key to a culture like the one that raised Western Digital out of the mud.

Western Digital had an operating system based on the 7 Habits detailed in Steven R. Covey's bestselling book *The 7 Habits of Highly Effective People*. By bringing this company the 7 Habits, we at FranklinCovey helped them instill a culture of proactivity and resourcefulness. Around eight thousand WD leaders and professionals had been trained in the 7 Habits; so their people were deeply rooted in a 7 Habits mindset long before the flood.

That's why the leaders could say, "Be Proactive," and WD's workers pitched in while others waited to be rescued.

That's why they could say, "First Things First," and the company was helping workers dig out of their own homes as well as recovering the factory.

That's why they could say, "Win-Win," and immediately spread the word that there would be no layoffs: "We win together or not at all."

Dave Rauch, senior vice president of Western Digital, said this: "We executed by tying our values to Covey's 7 *Habits of Highly Effective People*. WD's strong culture enabled the flawless crisis execution that resulted in the production facility's impressive recovery." When asked why Western Digital responded so differently from other companies swamped by the flood, another vice president, Dr. Sampan Silapadan, said, "The 7 Habits are the key. Everyone knows this."

The WD team succeeded because of the kind of people they are—and that is a reflection of the kind of leaders they have. Western Digital's highly effective leadership produced highly engaged people, and you can't calculate the value of that kind of engagement.

WD leaders did more than model leadership; they had made everyone a leader long before the flood. Employees were proactive, took ownership and responsibility, and acted accordingly when faced with a crisis. You, too, must make everyone leader, one who operates under the 7 Habits model. If you don't, you will lose the ultimate competitive advantage: people who bring talent, passion, determination, and focus to the success of the organization.

SIX KEY PRACTICES TO SUCCESS

At FranklinCovey, we've had thirty years' experience with hundreds of thousands of people in great companies, small schools, and whole departments of government. They come to us to gain insight and understanding of how to become highly effective organizations. We have six practices that show them how to do this, and it must begin with the essential mindsets—paradigms—that will enable them to thrive. We showed in Chapter 1 how the first shift in thinking is seeing that your people are your ultimate competitive advantage and that you must engage them before you can successfully move forward. We've also looked at how making everyone a leader and training them in the 7 Habits leads to a successful culture. Now it is time for you to shift your thinking in six key practice areas. Contrasted with the common practices of the past, these six highly effective practices compose the jobs you as a leader must do now:

COMMON PRACTICES	HIGHLY EFFECTIVE PRACTICES
1. Create and post mission statement in all public areas	1. Find and articulate the voice of the organization, and connect and align accordingly (aka "Lead with Purpose")
2. Develop a great strategy	2. Execute your strategy with excellence
3. Do more with less	3. Unleash and engage people to do infinitely more than you imagined they could
4. Become the provider/ employer of choice in your industry	4. Be the *most trusted* provider/ employer in your industry
5. "Create value" for customers	5. Help customers succeed by creating value
6. Satisfy customers	6. Create intense loyalty with customers

Why these six practices in particular? Each is based on fundamental principles that never change. The principles of proactivity, execution, productivity, and trust underlie every great achievement; nothing of lasting worth has ever been accomplished in human history without them. People who live by the opposite values—reactivity, aimless activity, waste, mistrust—contribute little to the success of the organization. The principles of mutual benefit and loyalty also underlie every successful relationship. People who live by the opposite values—indifference to others and disloyalty, for example—create no goodwill and work against the good of the organization. The common ways of thinking are often reactive and counterproductive; instead, we need this new model.

Consider: What kind of leader would you be if . . .

- no one but you felt a sense of responsibility for results?
- you didn't understand your own unique competitive advantage—the combined power of your team?
- you failed to execute some of your most important goals?
- you didn't fully leverage the genius, talent, and skill of your team?
- there was a lack of trust in you, between teammates, or in the organization?
- your customers had no clear idea of the unique value you bring to them?
- there was little loyalty on your team to you, each other, or the organization?

You can see for yourself why these paradigm shifts and new practices are vital. You can come up with many other success factors, but these six are inviolable. Leaders *must* be able to (1) find and articulate the "voice" of the organization, (2) execute with excellence, (3) unleash the productivity of people, (4) inspire trust, (5) help their customers succeed, and (6) engender loyalty in all stakeholders.

A paradigm is like an operating system for a computer. The machine will only do what the operating system allows it to do. If your paradigms are from the past, you'll be using obsolete applications that aren't up to the requirements of today.

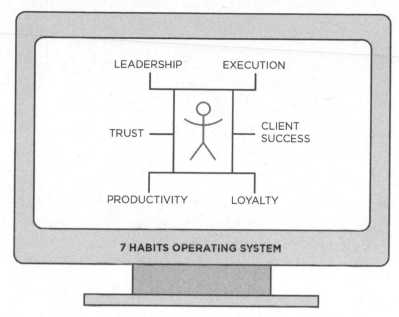

7 Habits Operating System

As the "7 Habits Operating System" graphic shows, you need an overarching "leadership operating system," like the framework laid out in *The 7 Habits of Highly Effective People*, to run today's applications—the paradigm shifts we've listed.

Each of these paradigm shifts and related practices is absolutely fundamental to success *now*. Each requires changing people's hearts and minds in fundamental ways, and changing behavior is about the hardest challenge anyone ever faces (if you don't think so, just consider how hard it is for you to change *your* behavior). It's a great challenge, but the shift must be made, and this book will show you how.

THE 7 HABITS OPERATING SYSTEM

So what are the features of this leadership operating system? What are the principles behind it? What are the attributes and behaviors of leaders who operate according to the 7 Habits?

- Proactive: They take initiative and responsibility for results (Habit 1).

- Purpose: They begin with the end in mind by having a sense of mission and vision that is clear, compelling, and infectious (Habit 2).

- Focused: They are highly productive and intensely focused on getting the right things done. They put first things first (Habit 3).

- Mutual Benefit: They "think win-win," showing deep respect and seeking always to benefit others as well as themselves (Habit 4).

- Communicators': They are profoundly empathic, seeking to understand people and issues and respectfully courageous when seeking to be understood (Habit 5).

- Synergistic: They value differences and collaborate to achieve the best possible results and outcomes (Habit 6).

- Continuously Improving: They demonstrate a personal and organizational commitment to continuous improvement and balance (Habit 7).

Obviously, anyone can have these attributes of a leader. It doesn't matter what your title or job description may be. This operating system or framework allows everyone at any level in the organization to know what is expected of them and to know how to succeed personally, interpersonally, and organizationally.

Years ago, Stephen R. Covey isolated these basic attributes as the 7 Habits. His book *The 7 Habits of Highly Effective People* swept like wildfire around the world, with millions of copies on millions of bookshelves everywhere, from pole to pole and from São Paulo to Saudi Arabia. The book's message lingers in many people's minds today because it has never lost its timeless appeal, and many organizational leaders have accepted the challenge of creating the conditions for turning everyone into a leader.

How do you make the 7 Habits everyone's personal operating system?

GIVEN A CHOICE, WOULD PEOPLE CHOOSE TO FOLLOW YOU?

The job starts with you—it's time to evaluate your own leadership operating system. Jim Collins has said, "One of the most important variables in whether an enterprise remains great lies in a simple question: What is the *truth* about the inner motivations, character, and ambition of those who hold power?"[1] That's why this book is first of all about you. Whether you realize it or not, you hold power. You can be the pivot point between the past and the future for your group, team, or organization. It doesn't matter if you are the most senior executive or the newest entry-level person. Regardless of your position, you can choose to lead and help create the future, or you can let the opportunity pass.

The real question is: What are *your* "inner motivations, character, and ambition"?

If you adopt the 7 Habits as your personal operating system, you can't help but become a leader. You'll behave the way a true leader behaves. But the 7 Habits are a matter of character: They operate from the inside out, which means you can't fake them on the surface. You can't pretend to be proactive or mission-driven or empathic with other people—they will spot your inconsistencies in a heartbeat. Practicing the 7 Habits means real introspection into your own character and motives. This doesn't mean you need to be perfect at living the 7 Habits. People will forgive lapses as long as they know you're trying.

To really understand the 7 Habits and how to incorporate them into your life, you need to read the book. We're not going into depth on each habit here. But let's look at the 7 Habits as a personal operating system for leaders.

HABIT 1—BE PROACTIVE: TAKE INITIATIVE AND RESPONSIBILITY FOR RESULTS

The first foundational habit of any true leader is to be proactive. It means that you habitually take responsibility. You take initiative. You act instead of waiting to be acted on. You're resourceful. You don't take no for an answer (at least not until there's absolutely no way to get a yes). You act on the basis of your values rather than simply responding to the stimuli in your life.

Proactivity is a simple yet profound principle, but many people have trouble with it. It's easier to be reactive and live on inertia than to stand up and lead. We're uncomfortable with change and the people who want to change things. We discount our own abilities ("I'm not a natural leader," "I don't know what to do," "I don't have any influence around here").

The Wall Street Journal observes, "Most managers will spend their entire work life reacting to orders from above, reacting to pressures and problems from below, or simply reacting to the insistent demands of a busy workplace . . . If all you do is react, you will fail as a manager. You may be good at solving problems that arise. You may be skilled at responding to the needs and requests of those you work for, or the people on your team. You may work long hours, be loved and respected by your employees, and be the very model of organizational efficiency. But you will not be an effective manager."[2]

Effective leaders are proactive, not reactive. They are passion-driven and resourceful, and they find a way to achieve what matters most.

In the film *Dead Poets Society,* a group of boys starts classes at a private school in New England. On the first day, the wide-eyed and anxious boys proceed in a very orderly way from chemistry class to Latin to trigonometry, listening quietly to the standard initiation speeches from each teacher. Finally, they meet their new English teacher, Mr. Keating. He asks a boy to open the literature textbook and read aloud the introduction, a dry essay on the science of interpreting poetry. As the boy reads, it becomes clear that Mr. Keating doesn't like what he's hearing. He then stops the boy and asks him to rip the introduction out of the book.

The boys stare at him in amazement. He then orders them all to rip those pages from their books, as if the very presence of the essay alongside the works of Keats and Blake and Wordsworth and Shakespeare threatens their power and meaning. The teacher gathers the boys close to him and in a hushed, dramatic tone, declares, "We don't read and write poetry because it is cute. We read and write poetry because we are members of the human race. And the human race is filled with passion!"

Being passionate is the essence of leadership. There is a science of leadership, but it's secondary to the hunger and thirst leaders have to make a difference, to make a contribution that matters. If you are not passionately engaged in your work, you might ask yourself why. If others are not passionately engaged, it's essential to find out why.

> While proactive people are passionate, they are also resourceful. Proactivity means you *find a way.*

Great leaders have the "passion to see it through," as Seth Godin says. They have "the willingness to find a different route when the first one doesn't work. The certainty that in fact, there is a way, and you care enough to find it . . . This is a choice, not something you

. . . get certified in."[3] While proactive people are passionate, they are also resourceful. Proactivity means you *find a way.*

More than a century ago, a young African American woman named Mary McLeod Bethune started the Literary and Industrial Training School for Negro Girls in Daytona Beach, Florida. The fifteenth child of former slaves, Mary grew up in deep poverty, but with her passion for learning, she pleaded for a place in school and eventually became a teacher. Recognizing that black girls of that time and place had little opportunity for an education, she became fired up with the idea of starting her own school for them.

Mary's cash resources consisted of a dollar and a half, but that didn't stop her. Her resources were limited only by her ingenuity, and that was unlimited. The only place she could find for her school was a shack next to the town dump, so she cleaned it up and used it. There was no money for supplies, so she made desks out of old boxes, pencils from charred wood, and ink out of boiled-down berry juice. Her desk was a packing case. "I lay awake nights, contriving how to make peach baskets into chairs,"[4] she said.

The school opened in 1904 with five eager girls, six books, and the devoted Mary McLeod Bethune as the teacher. While teaching reading, writing, and math, she also taught them to be as resourceful as she was. What could they do to help support the school? One girl knew how to make a mattress by stuffing it with moss. Others knew how to bake pies. So they made and sold mattresses to their neighbors, and they offered pieces of sweet potato pie to the tourists who descended on Daytona Beach for the auto races. That's how they paid the $11 monthly rent on their school. "I considered cash money as the smallest part of my resources," Mary later wrote. "I had faith in a loving God, faith in myself, and a desire to serve."[5] Mary's little school eventually grew into Bethune-Cookman University, thriving today with nearly 4,000 students and a $34 million endowment.

No one who knows the story of Mary McLeod Bethune can talk with a straight face about being short on resources. Our own ingenuity is the greatest of our resources, but only proactive people can leverage that resource. How resourceful are you? How resourceful are the people around you? Or do you live in a culture of helplessness, constantly restrained by a lack of passion and resources from the great contribution you are capable of making?

HABIT 2—BEGIN WITH THE END IN MIND: GAIN A CLEAR SENSE OF MISSION

The second foundational habit of any true leader is to have a clear end in mind—a vision or mission that inspires and energizes you. It also means that you have a clear purpose in mind for everything you do—initiatives, projects, and meetings. It's based on the simple principle of knowing your destination early; even if you fall short, you'll be moving in the right direction.

Some people say, "All this talk about vision is just drivel." In fact, there's a popular myth that when the legendary Lou Gerstner took over a floundering IBM, he said, "The last thing IBM needs is a vision." He has since said he was misunderstood: "I said we didn't need a vision *right now*. IBM had file drawers full of vision statements." What was clear to him was that IBM wasn't *acting* on its vision. "We weren't getting the job done."[6]

> Our own ingenuity is the greatest of our resources, but only proactive people can leverage that resource.

Everything made by humans is the result of a vision, from a potato peeler to the *Mona Lisa*. It's designed in the mind first. Ironically, we know how to design potato peelers, but we're not very good at designing a life. By just taking things as they come, we go at the most important things in life without much vision.

How often do we hear (and sometimes say), "They don't know what they're doing in the head office! This organization is drifting. Does anybody know where we're headed?" Companies engrave empty, big-headed mission statements on bronze tablets: "Our mission is to maximize shareholder value," "We exist to serve our customers with excellence," "We endeavor to provide value-added solutions to exceed our customers' expectations by continuously improving our unique integrated resources to stay competitive in the global marketplace of tomorrow." So many mission statements are like these—void of passion, vision, or even sense. As Justin Fox, editorial director of *The Harvard Business Review,* wrote in *The Atlantic,* "It can be awfully hard to motivate employees or entice customers with the motto 'We maximize shareholder value.'"[7]

It sounds so obvious: What is our real mission? Do we even have a mission? If so, does it make sense? Is there any passion at all, any aspiration in it? How will we measure success? It's remarkable how many managers never even ask these basic questions; and if they do think about them they're afraid to ask because, after all, they should know, shouldn't they?

Even fewer ask themselves, "What is my own personal mission? What should I contribute here? What kind of a difference do I want to make? What will I remember about my work here? How will people remember me—or will they remember me at all?" Or do they see themselves as "job descriptions with legs," giving little or nothing of their own minds and hearts to their work?

"The human race is filled with passion," Mr. Keating said to the boys in *Dead Poets Society.* "But poetry, beauty, romance, love, these are what we stay alive for." He then asks, as did the great Walt Whitman, 'The powerful play goes on and you may contribute a verse.'* What will your verse be?"

What a wonderful and appropriate question for each of us to consider. What will our individual verses be? How will we make our contributions to the world?

Creating—or better said, *discovering*—your personal mission is a difficult but very powerful process. It will help bring clarity to the

---

*from "Oh Me! Oh Life!" by Walt Whitman, *Leaves of Grass*, 1892 things you value, and will help define how you spend your time and the contributions you will make. It will bring a greater sense of meaning to your work. You'll be able to help your team craft its mission. You might even influence your organization's mission.

When Mary McLeod Bethune was campaigning for her school, she bravely introduced herself at a palatial vacation home in Daytona Beach and was received by the old gentleman who owned it. He enjoyed her gift of sweet potato pie and kept asking her back, which delighted her. She talked about her school in radiant terms, about the library and chapel and the schoolrooms and the lovely, uniformed girls. "I would like you to become one of the school's trustees," she told him.

One day his big limousine arrived unannounced at the school. The old gentleman got out, looked around, and saw nothing but a shed in a muddy field. One girl read aloud from a geography book while others peeled and boiled sweet potatoes for pie. Mary took off her apron and looked the man straight in the eye.

"And where is this school that you wanted me to be a trustee of?" he asked. He was obviously not pleased.

Mary smiled up at him and said, "In my mind and in my soul."

After a moment's hesitation, James Norris Gamble, the fabulously wealthy inventor of Ivory soap, wrote her a check. Overwhelmed by the power of her vision, Gamble provided her the means for realizing that vision for the rest of his life.

But the Bethune school was only a part of her vision. "The drums of Africa still beat in my heart," she said. "They will not let me rest while there is a single Negro boy or girl without a chance to prove his worth."[8] With Gamble's support and that of many others, Mary McLeod Bethune served as a remarkable agent of change for African American people. She helped found the National Association of Colored Women to help black people register to vote (which earned her a few visits from the Ku Klux Klan). She also became the first African American female head of a US federal agency, the Division of Negro Affairs, as a close advisor to President Franklin D. Roosevelt and his wife, Eleanor. Finally, she was the only black woman present at the founding of the United Nations.

Again, Habit 2 starts with you. What is your mission or vision of your own future? What will your contribution be in your current work role? Once you have discovered and carefully defined your personal mission, you will have a clear "end in mind" and you can begin to influence others to make their contributions, as Mary McLeod Bethune did.

Jack Welch said, "Good business leaders create a vision, articulate the vision, passionately own the vision, and relentlessly drive it to completion." Your leadership starts with showing people "where you are going, what your dream looks like, where we are going to be when successful."[9]

HABIT 3—PUT FIRST THINGS FIRST: FOCUS ON GETTING THE RIGHT THINGS DONE

The third foundational habit of any true leader is to prioritize so you're giving the most and best attention to what's most important. This is easy to do if you already know what the mission is; without the mission, you can't tell what the most important things are.

And that's the problem with many leaders. Because they're unclear on the end state or destination, they can't distinguish between what is "wildly important" and what is merely an "urgent priority." Many so-called urgent priorities are neither urgent nor priorities; they are momentary distractions that actually prevent leaders from achieving the mission.

On a hot September day in 2005, a wildfire erupted in Topanga Canyon, California. Only a mountain ridge separated the huge fire from Los Angeles, and a major disaster seemed likely. One of America's largest cities could have been consumed, but it wasn't. The

damage was limited because the Los Angeles County Fire Department had long since "put first things first."

Most people would say that the mission of a fire department is
to put out fires. The L.A. County Fire Department didn't see it that
way—their mission was to prevent damage to life
and property. They didn't want to fight *any* fires;
they never wanted to deal with a fire at all. So long
before the wildfire, they adopted aggressive goals:
educating the public about making "defensible
space" around their homes, clearing brush, remov-
ing fire hazards, and creating safe zones. They
had pursued this goal intently, and as a result the
Topanga Canyon Fire was far less destructive than it might have been.
The department never has to fight a fire they've already prevented.

> **What is more
> important than
> fighting a fire?
> *Preventing the fire
> in the first place.***

By contrast, most leaders spend most of their time "fighting fires."
You hear it all the time—people are "insanely busy" trying to keep
up with urgent demands on their time and never catching up, never
getting on top of it all.

So what is more important than fighting a fire? *Preventing the fire
in the first place.*

That's the "first thing" that needs to be put first. If the mission is
to preserve life and property, the goal must be not to fight fires but to
keep them from breaking out.

As *The Wall Street Journal* says, "'What should we do?' is the first
question the manager must answer. 'What is the mission of the organization I am managing? What is the strategy for accomplishing that
mission? What are my goals for the future, consistent with strategy
and mission? What are the overall goals for my team, and for each
member of the team?'"[10] Once the mission is clear (Habit 2), the leader's job is to set and execute on clear goals for achieving it (Habit 3).

Remember the principle of "no involvement, no commitment."
When a leader merely dictates the team's purpose without involving
others in the process, that leader will find a low level of commitment

and a high level of burnout from others. At the same time, leaders can't just rely on the input of others as the sole basis of their direction. A leader is more than a census taker. It's impossible to please all the people all the time, so don't even try. Involve people in key decisions, let them help you clarify the direction of the team or the initiative, but be prepared to take a stand once you have gathered data and input. Your shared mission is your guide to determining what truly are the "first things."

So what are your "first things"? What goals must you set to achieve your mission? Just as important, what goals can you say no to?

HABIT 4—THINK WIN/WIN: PROVIDE MUTUAL BENEFIT BY RESPECTFULLY SEEKING TO BENEFIT OTHERS AS WELL AS YOURSELF

The fourth foundational habit of any true leader is to think win-win. The basic principle here is respect for others *and* for yourself. No arrangement in the business world—or in life, actually—can succeed unless all parties are winning, especially in the long term.

"But business is all about competition," you say. "Whenever a customer makes a choice, somebody wins and somebody loses." And you're right, in independent situations—one side "wins." But even in classically competitive situations, there are opportunities for interdependence. For example, airlines want you to buy their seats, but most will send you to another airline if a mechanical issue comes up. Virtually everything you do and every relationship you have depends on helping someone else succeed.

When the global banking crisis hit in 2008, it became almost impossible to get credit. David Fishwick, a prosperous dealer in minibuses, saw his business dry up overnight. Dave had spent his life building up his business and the town of Burnley in the north of

England. "I had a lot of customers who bought minibuses on finance and who were decent, reliable, hardworking people that always paid back anything they owed," he said "Suddenly, the credit crunch hit and these people I'd known for years couldn't get a penny from the banks."

Burnley, already struggling with 13 percent unemployment, was about to hit the wall. "Everywhere I looked, businesses were going bust and shops were sitting empty with big 'to let' signs over the door," Dave said. "Every time a business goes bust, other businesses lose their customers, which pushes them even closer to the edge. The problem was that there was no money to get things moving and the banks certainly weren't doing anything to help." It was "lose-lose" everywhere you looked. But Dave Fishwick, a proactive, visionary leader, had a win-win mentality, and he decided to apply to open his own bank for the people of Burnley. "Why not?" he thought.

The government told him why not. Under the law, he needed a vast set-aside of millions of pounds before he could get a bank charter. Like any good proactive leader, he refused to take no for an answer and found a loophole: He could have his bank if he didn't *call* it a bank. So he adopted the slogan "Bank on Dave!" and set up shop. Dave's entire philosophy is win-win: He pays his depositors much higher interest than they can get from a bank, which draws enthusiastic customers. He gets to know every borrower personally and guarantees every loan he makes. So far his trust has paid off—only 2 percent of the loans he's made are in arrears (traditional banks, which are seeing around 9 or 10 percent, would love those results).

For example, the Turners, a couple struggling to start a catering business, couldn't get a loan from any bank. They went to Dave and he lent them the £8,500 they needed; but he did more than that. He advised them on their marketing and advertising, introduced them around to local businesses, and helped them set up a sandwich stand at a big construction site. The result: They attracted a lot of customers. As the Turners said, "We couldn't have done it without the loan and Dave's advice. He opened our eyes to what can be done." And, of course, they are repaying Bank on Dave in full and on time.

In the world of Dave Fishwick, everybody wins—his depositors, his borrowers, and the local economy. He wins, too: "If nobody could buy a new minibus, that would mean no more David Fishwick Minibuses!" He is helping turn a lose-lose situation into a win-win success story.[11]

Dave understands the basic leadership principle of abundance— you don't succeed unless others succeed, too, and therefore win-win is the only rational way for a leader to think. Do you consider yourself a "win-win thinker"? What evidence do you have? Would other people say that about you? Do you work in a win-win culture?

HABIT 5—SEEK FIRST TO UNDERSTAND, THEN TO BE UNDERSTOOD: EMPATHIZE IN ORDER TO UNDERSTAND PEOPLE AND THEIR PERSPECTIVES BEFORE SHARING YOUR OWN

The fifth foundational habit of any true leader is to seek first to understand other people before you try to make yourself understood. The basic principle here is *empathy*—listening with the intent to fully understand what they are feeling and saying. This allows a leader to get to the heart of the matter whether they agree or not.

Why is empathy a crucial habit for a leader?

Picture a business leader with no empathy for her customers. How long will she stay in business if she remains totally disconnected from their needs? How about a project leader with no empathy for his stakeholders or team members? Or a teacher with no empathy for his students? An aeronautical engineer with no empathy for the passengers on the plane she's designing? A hospital administrator with no empathy for the patients?

Obviously, most leaders already have some empathy—the problem is not that they can't understand people, but that they feel they must solve all their problems. Leaders have a compulsion at best to fix everything and at worst to smooth things over. It's a natural urge to want to jump in and save the day, to be the answer to everyone's problems. Of course it's important to get to a solution, but you can't solve a problem you don't understand.

"I don't have time to listen," says the typical, notorious alpha leader. "I already know what the problem is and I know how to solve it. My brain is way ahead of theirs. Time is precious—why should I waste it sitting and listening to people?"

By contrast, when asked, "What advice would you give to a new chief executive?" the remarkable Angela Ahrendts, former CEO of Burberry, has a one-word answer: "Listen." And what is the greatest mistake a leader can make? "Not listening."

Under Ahrendts' leadership, Burberry moved from a declining brand that had lost its appeal to a world leader in the high-end clothing market. Burberry revenues have tripled to more than $3 billion and shares have tripled in value. Burberry fashion shows draw a million viewers on YouTube and the company has fifteen million followers on Facebook, making Burberry the leading luxury brand in the world.[12] Clearly, Angela Ahrendts knows something about leadership.

For Ahrendts, listening with empathy is the key leadership skill. "Just listen, just learn, just feel. It's tough for type-A personalities to do that in this position, but you'll be better off in the long run," she says.

> Great leaders allow empathy to shape the vision . . . Your goal is to understand.

The resurgence of Burberry was totally unexpected, as the brand had been hijacked by counterfeiters and knockoffs—the famous Burberry plaid essentially meant nothing anymore. Angela quietly listened, putting herself in the position of the Burberry customer: "Where are the great old trench coats Burberry was famous for?" She listened to the sales force: "We can't make near the commission on a stack of polo shirts as we can on one trench coat." She listened to Millennials: "We want to see it online. We want to click on it and buy it *now*." By reaching out to understand, Ahrendts knew what to do. She swept away hundreds of mediocre products, resurrected the chic, beautiful Burberry outerwear, and put the whole company online, sponsoring the first YouTube 3D fashion show in history. Burberry took off.[13]

Many new leaders start by imposing their vision on people, but great leaders allow empathy to shape the vision. "If I had implemented everything that I thought about the first thirty or sixty days, I can't imagine where we'd be," Ahrendts says. "The biggest mistake a leader can make is not listening, not feeling, not using your team. You hire functional experts for a reason. If I go to another country I hire an interpreter. If I go to court I hire somebody to defend me. It's no different in business." Why have a team if you're not going to leverage what they have to contribute?

You practice Habit 5 just by listening—nothing else. You listen without interrupting, without judging, analyzing, or answering back in your head. You're not thinking about what you're going to say next. Instead, you're listening closely both to what the person is saying and to what they're feeling.

Your goal is to understand. If you're a leader, that's your job. You can't connect with customers and colleagues without empathy and understanding. Only by getting into others' shoes can you serve them in a customized way—the way *they* want to be served.

Empathy becomes even more crucial as leaders deal with a global marketplace. For example, empathy is extremely important in the Chinese workplace, where a leader is expected to interact daily with employees and customers. While Western Hemisphere CEOs can lock themselves in their offices for days on end, managers in China pay far more personal attention to staff and colleagues. As one expert says, "In China, leadership is a contact sport."[14]

A European company with a joint venture in China sent them a leader with an excellent track record but no experience outside Europe. He was a good "numbers" man but a poor listener, paying little attention to the people around him. As *McKinsey Quarterly* described him, "The executive did not care about their observations and ideas, expected the staff only to follow his instructions, and did not listen to customer feedback. After two years, the executive was replaced, but the damage was done and the operation closed eighteen months later."[15]

Only an empathic leader can unleash the potential of other people. Leaders without empathy are literally working in the dark because they're ignorant of their team members' passions, talents, and skills. You can't possibly discover and capitalize on the motivations of another human being without knowing the person deeply. For instance, as Professor Heidi Grant Halvorson says, some people eagerly embrace big, grand goals, while others are wary and skeptical, preferring more vigilance and less risk. Unless you know the "motivational fit" of each team member, you'll make poor choices about engaging their unique skills and talent. The only way to uncover that motivational fit is to listen and understand.[16]

Empathy is essential to effective leadership, and it can't be faked. Stephen R. Covey said, "Leaders who take an interest in people merely because they should will be both wrong and unsuccessful. They will be wrong because regard for people is an end in itself. They will be unsuccessful because they will be found out."

For many, empathy is counterintuitive. In fact, among the hundreds of thousands of people we have assessed on various leadership and effectiveness principles, this is the least practiced and, not surprisingly, most requested skill.

On a pragmatic level, full understanding earns the leader the right to be understood in return. Leaders can confidently share their perspective and align it to what they learned from their colleagues' perspective.

HABIT 6—SYNERGIZE: LEVERAGE THE GIFTS AND RESOURCES OF OTHER PEOPLE

The sixth foundational habit of any true leader is to synergize with other people. The basic principle here is *the whole is greater than the sum of the parts.* A team of people with diverse skills and perspectives is always more productive and creative than each member alone can be, not to mention the lone leader trying to figure things out in isolation. One plus one equals three, or ten, or a thousand. Consider: How many pounds can one draft horse pull? Answer: About 1,000 pounds. How many pounds can two draft horses pull? Answer: about 4,000 pounds. In this case, 1 + 1 = 4. That's simple math that is not always so simple. Why this result? By pulling together, each horse compensates for the other's weaknesses. They complement each other; they fill in performance gaps. Each horse on its own is powerful. Together, their strength is remarkable!

We all pay lots of lip service to diversity, but in practice leaders tend to be territorial and defensive. Everyone hails the new merger for its "synergy," but most mergers fail because synergy isn't allowed to happen. (Marriages generally fail for the same reason.)

> No individual is like any other—each has gifts, talents, passion, and skills no one else can duplicate. Effective leaders leverage those differences.

A large European construction firm wanted a presence in North America and acquired a cement company in the American South. Everyone looked forward to the synergies; the numbers looked wonderful, and the capabilities of the two firms fit together well. But year after year, performance fell further until the CEO turned in desperation to a study group from the Sloan School of Management at MIT to get to the root of the problem.

Their conclusion: "The anticipated economic synergies have not materialized because little attention has been paid to achieving psychological synergies." They reported "open hostility" among the people in the acquired company; they "hated" their European owners and would not share data with them or even allow them on the premises without permission from their own CEO. "The goal of a merger is to have the component parts add up to more than they are worth individually," the study group observed. "Obviously, this hasn't happened."[17]

Probing further, the study group found that the parent company didn't value the very different culture, ideas, and input of the people at the acquired company. While the acquirer had hoped these people's potential would be unleashed, they felt chained down instead.

When titles are conferred on people, they tend to become over-controlling without realizing it. Their identity gets tied up in the phrase "I'm in charge here." They value sameness, so they squelch ideas from the members of their team. They want order, so they enforce uniformity of opinion. They want their way, so they discount the divergent views of the team—and synergy is suppressed.

The great irony here is that synergy is the reason for having a team in the first place. No individual is like any other—each has gifts, talents, passion, and skills no one else can duplicate. Effective leaders leverage those differences.

Consider what happens when Airbus puts together a team of biologists, physiologists, artists, molecular physicists, graphic designers, and psychologists (and an aeronautical engineer or two) in a room and asks them to come up with the airplane of the future. What they envision will completely revolutionize air travel.

Imagine an airplane that mimics a human skeleton—it can twist, turn, spring, and vault like an athlete. Instead of wearing out, the plane's muscular shell actually gets stronger with stress, just like human muscles do. Its parts look like human bones; the mechanism of a baggage compartment is modeled on your shoulder joints. When you sit down, your seat molds itself around your body to give you a customized ride. Instead of a dim, dense atmosphere, the cabin is spacious and bathed in natural light: The skin of the airplane transmits light and energy and even data, carrying music, video, and virtual golf games to the passengers. And the entire plane is organically grown from nanotubes—an enormous 3D printout weighing half of what our most advanced airplanes weigh.

"The airplane of the future will get its own consciousness," the designers say. "It will be more like a living organism than just a collection of very complex technology."[18]

This is the power of a synergistic team, where each individual member's skills and genius and energies are leveraged to produce a marvel that no one could produce alone. On this team, every member is a leader.

"Wait," you say. "How can everybody on a team be a leader?"

Imagine a team where everyone is a leader, where every member is proactive and visionary with clearly shared priorities. Imagine a team where everyone is looking out for the interests of one another, where they are intensely empathic and open to different views—in short, a team where the 7 Habits are the operating system. That is the team you need *now*.

Do you tend to welcome different points of view or discourage them? Are you territorial, defensive, or closed to the ideas of others? Are you suffering from the "not invented here" syndrome? Or is your team a model of synergy? Do team members feel unleashed or chained down?

HABIT 7—SHARPEN THE SAW: KEEP GETTING BETTER AND MORE CAPABLE, NEVER STANDING STILL

The seventh foundational habit of a true leader is to continuously improve your capabilities instead of letting them wear out. It's based on the principle that if you neglect yourself, your physical health, your learning, and your relationships, you will become dull and use-less, like an overused saw. Of course, any organization that doesn't continuously improve its capabilities will inevitably fade away, but continuous improvement starts with you. The whole mindset behind Stephen R. Covey's "sharpen the saw" habit is that continual learning and growth are as essential to the individual as to the firm.

Moulinex, once the biggest maker of household appliances in Europe, died a protracted death because it neglected to sharpen the saw. The company rose after World War II from the small workshop of Jean Mantelet, the inventor of the food processor, and by the 1970s had become a true industrial giant. Its assembly lines employed thousands of unskilled workers. Money poured into its coffers.

But because its leaders stopped learning, Moulinex stopped learning. The leaders assumed that their industrial model would go on unchanged forever and settled back to collect the revenue. Meanwhile, hungry companies in Southeast Asia were copying Moulinex prod-ucts and making them even better and cheaper, using new quality-management techniques to minimize costs and maximize quality. As their once-global markets dried up, the leaders of Moulinex sat pas-sively and looked the other way. By 2001, the giant was bankrupt, a classic victim of failure to sharpen the saw.[19]

"Okay," you say, "they asked for it. That's not our mindset here. We're flexible, nimble, alert to change, and constantly improving everything we do."

If that's true, then you are the exception. A global survey of com-panies in all major industries found that more than 60 percent have tried and failed to implement continuous improvement systems, and that doesn't even count those who haven't tried. Those who have succeeded cite leadership commitment as by far the major reason for their success, and those who have failed overwhelmingly point to (surprise!) leaders' lack of commitment as the cause of the failure (88 percent!).[20]

Do you work for a "sharpen the saw" organization? Does your own team have a systematic approach to improving what you do? Do you have evidence that your core processes are getting better all the time?

And what about yourself—are you mentally and physically sharp? Are you a "continuous learner"? Do you work to keep your most important relationships healthy?

LET EVERYONE LEAD

Your first steps to building a winning culture that has embraced the 7 Habits and holds the ultimate competitive advantage are to adopt the mindset that everyone on your team can lead and accept that it's your job to make them a leader, to inspire them to embrace their roles. You do this by establishing a framework—the operating system we've mentioned—for getting the job done effectively. This framework is ubiquitous and not role-specific. It demands that you "show up" and model the culture rather than talk about it in generic terms (or worse yet, "talk at" team members about it). It will develop high-character and high-competence leaders at every level of the organization. It will give everyone a common language and a set of behaviors they can depend on as they work to achieve results year after year.

> Leadership is a choice, not just a position.

Designing Your Culture Deliberately

Is your organizational culture working for you or against you? We invite you to design your culture deliberately. How much time and energy do we devote to strategic plans and initiatives, KPIs, goals, and project planning? Have you ever ignored or forgotten to address culture during a key strategic shift? Ever experienced a culture pushing back on a strategy or a changed management initiative? We recall hearing a devoted long-term public servant speaking to her team in the hallway after a new political leader's election and "inspiring call-to-action" speech. She started the sentence off with, "Be respectful, and know that we can wait out any of this leader's strategies . . . we've done it before and we can do it again." That's culture speaking back. Too often we leave it to chance and it pushes back hard.

A great culture must be leader-led and designed intentionally, and must have an established framework of behaviors and language that engages and aligns the performance of everyone in the organization. Everyone knows how to win. Everyone leads. Can you imagine if everyone in your organization behaved like a leader? What results would that enable?

> You will never capture people's hearts by treating them like jackasses—yet that's how most leaders try to lead.

The ultimate competitive advantage will go to those who adopt the paradigm that everyone on your team should be a leader. Too many see leadership as a position. But leadership is a choice, not just a position. Like the soccer players on Coach Dorrance's winning team, each member of your team can take ownership of something. Each member can feel that they are making a worthwhile contribution.

How to Effectively Change Behaviors

The typical way to change people's behavior is to reward or threaten them. This is what Stephen R. Covey called "the great jackass theory of human motivation—carrot and stick." The problem with this approach is that it treats people like animals, and it works only on the surface and only temporarily. Like Tom, people who are threatened develop a paradigm of fear, and so they act out of fear. They will "work" for a company, but they will never give it their hearts. They will never speak honestly, contribute freely, or do more than is required.

They will never, ever tell you what they really think.

Yes, they will be motivated, all right—motivated to evade responsibility—but they will never be inspired. In today's workplace, so many workers are afraid, and they act like it. They take little initiative, they avoid responsibility, they keep their thoughts to themselves—and they bring as little as possible to the table so they won't get in trouble. This is the legacy of the Industrial Age, and it's still with us. You will never capture people's hearts by treating them like jackasses—yet that's how most leaders try to lead.

> That's the purpose of this book: to replace unproductive paradigms with inspiring new paradigms and corresponding practices that will unleash new and extraordinarily productive behavior.

The secret to changing behavior is to change paradigms and enact highly effective practices built upon these new ways of thinking. And that's the purpose of this book: to replace unproductive paradigms with inspiring new paradigms and corresponding practices that will unleash new and extraordinarily productive behavior. That's *the job that you must do now.*

The story of Western Digital proves that this job, while challenging, can be done, and that the results are dramatic. FranklinCovey partnered with this world leader in storage solutions to reach that ultimate competitive level, and we can help you, too.

Leaders as Owners

The most highly motivated people in any organization tend to be its leaders. They are the people who are responsible for results—they

HUMANIZERS VS. SYSTEMIZERS

Stanford professor Harold Leavitt beautifully described today's leadership dilemma this way: "'Humanizers' focus on the people side of the organization, on human needs, attitudes, and emotions. They are generally opposed to hierarchies, viewing them as restrictive, spirit-draining, even imprisoning. 'Systemizers,' in contrast, fixate on facts, measurements, and systems. They are generally in favor of hierarchies, treating them as effective structures for doing big jobs. Humanizers tend to stereotype systemizers as insensitive, anal-retentive types who think that if they can't measure it, it isn't there. Systemizers tend to caricature humanizers as fuzzy-headed, over-emotional creatures who don't think straight."[21]

Most intelligent managers vacillate between the two as they develop a sense about which style to use in a given situation. Some try for a balance between boss and best friend, but it's an extremely tough balance to strike. So managers keep seesawing between the styles. Somebody's floundering over there, so you have to go micromanage them. Meanwhile, everybody else feels abandoned, and other people start to flounder, and eventually you're micromanaging *them*. And so it goes, as you run from one crisis to another.

Professor Leavitt concluded that this typical approach to organizational leadership "breeds infantilizing dependency, distrust, conflict, toadying, territoriality, distorted communication, and most of the other human ailments that plague every large organization."[22]

The problem, however, is not how to strike a balance between two dysfunctional styles of leading people—the problem is in your paradigm of a *leader.*

"own" the results, good or bad, so they're highly committed to producing the best results possible.

People who own things take care of them—they wash their cars, repair their homes, tend their gardens. They *take* care *because* they care. On the other hand, non-owners care little, if at all—who washes a rental car?

In organizations, the leaders are owners—of goals, projects, initiatives, and systems. A big challenge for leaders is to get other people—the non-owners—to care about those things. But followers, no matter how well compensated, no matter the promises, perks, or promotions, simply don't care in the same way that leaders do. Followers don't *own* anything.

> A title doesn't automatically "en-title" you to anything.

Attempts after the middle of the last century to establish "participatory management," originally intended to flatten hierarchies and make organizations more democratic, didn't work. Just the opposite happened as hierarchies became more entrenched, silos popped up everywhere, turf wars became the norm, and politics nosed into the relationships between leaders and followers.

In our culture, leaders have always been defined by their titles. But as Stephen R. Covey said, "I don't define leadership as becoming the CEO. A CEO is no more likely to be a leader than anyone else." What Covey meant was, a grant of formal authority doesn't make you a leader. Owning a title makes you accountable, but it doesn't make you a leader any more than owning a pair of skis makes you a downhill racer. A title doesn't automatically "en-title" you to anything.

Think about leadership in two ways: formal authority that comes with a title, and moral authority that comes with your character. As you look at the leaders you've known, you know some of them have had little influence despite their titles. Then there are the unofficial leaders everybody trusts.

The truth is, anyone can be a leader regardless of title or job description. Gandhi energized the entire Indian nation and won its independence, but never held a formal title. Every organization has an informal network of "go-to people" for wisdom, advice, and solutions. They are often neither officers nor managers, but they have earned informal authority because of their experience and influence.

In fact, having only a few leaders deciding everything just bottlenecks the whole organization. This is not news, but little has been done to change things. Management expert Gary Hamel says, "We still have these organizations where too much power and authority are reserved for people at the top of the pyramid . . . We have to syndicate the work of leadership more broadly."[23]

Everyone Leads

So . . . if you want to motivate people, and you want your team to take ownership of their work, *why not make everyone a leader?*

It's entirely possible to create the conditions where everyone can be a leader if you change your paradigm of what a leader is. When you no longer think of leadership as the sole province of a few select people, you realize that all people have primary leadership qualities that can be leveraged. Initiative, resourcefulness, vision, strategic focus, creativity—these qualities are in no way limited to the executive suite.

> You could argue that the main job of leaders is to create other leaders.

You could argue that the main job of leaders is to create other leaders. That's how Jack Welch saw his job at General Electric: "The challenge is to move the sense of ownership . . . down through the organization," he says. Dee Hock, the legendary founder of Visa, believed that leadership should be everyone's job, a "360-degree" job, where everyone leads down, up, and around through their individual contributions and influence. According to

Stanford University's landmark study on CEO effectiveness, "Focusing on developing the next generation of leadership is essential to planning beyond the next quarter and avoiding the short-term thinking that inhibits growth."[24]

But if everyone's a leader, you ask, who are the followers? That's easy. It's like asking, "When it comes to shopping, who are the buyers and who are the sellers?" Everyone is both. The same person sells *and* buys, and in an organization the same person leads *and* follows.

What does it mean to have a culture where everyone is a leader?

It means that there's a common leadership operating system, a framework, that everyone in the organization shares. Your devices have an operating system that makes everything else run; without it your devices are just dead pieces of plastic. In the same way, your work has standard operating procedures, and your organization has a certain way of leading and behaving.

What is your leadership operating system? Does everyone in the organization know how to succeed? How to behave? How to problem-solve and innovate?

As we've seen, in most organizations the current leadership operating system is flawed. Some are deeply flawed, where only big egos, tyrants, or passive-aggressives can thrive. But most leaders simply have an outdated paradigm. They're doing their best to take charge instead of inspiring others to take charge.

Looking at the early structure of information technology is helpful here. In the old world, a big, master mainframe computer dictated to subservient computers, which simply did as they were told. That day is long gone. Now we all have our own smartphones, laptops, tablets—all connected to clouds brimming with information (much of which didn't even exist yesterday) that we can access with the swipe of a finger.

Similarly, to be "the leader" traditionally means to take the whole enterprise on your back—to be the mainframe. It's an exhausting prospect. It's also terribly ineffective, to say the least. Here you are, surrounded by people with enormous talent, capability, experience, insight, and ingenuity, while you pretend to be the sole source of those things. We're still "leading" others as if we were back in an Industrial Age world. But now we've reached a tipping point where that paradigm just won't work. It's time for a totally new leadership operating system that frees *everyone* to lead.

Sue, who constantly travels for work, tells about an extraordinary leader she has met, Captain Denny Flanagan of United Airlines, and how he exemplifies the strategy and benefits of letting employees be leaders and owners. In this world where air travel is so often such a trial, she says no one treats passengers the way this leader does:

"At the end of a miserable twenty hours in an overcrowded gate at the Chicago airport, he was the captain who would either get us to Orange County before the airport closed for the night—or not. The timing was critical and really tight. I was mesmerized when he took the microphone and rallied all the passengers. He told us he knew we had experienced a horrible day full of delays, and he wanted to keep the airline's promise to get us to California; but he would need all of our help if we were to take off before the window closed in California.

> "He knows that every time he walks onto an airplane, he has the opportunity to commit, model, and demonstrate what excellence looks like."

"The next thing I knew the passengers were lining up, helping each other with kids, strollers, walkers—the plane was boarded more efficiently than I have ever seen, and cheerfully by every passenger. The flight attendants saw the captain holding babies, helping passengers get on, and loading their luggage, and they followed suit. About two hours into the flight I received a personal note from him thanking me for my loyalty. I still have it.

"In years of flying and millions of miles, I have never seen another airline pilot do what he did that night. I stayed on the plane after landing to meet Denny and to thank him for the best flight of my life. I will never forget him telling me that he basically discovered that his job was to 'create a culture' every three to six hours. He knows that every time he walks onto an airplane, he has the opportunity to commit, model, and demonstrate what excellence looks like. He also has a firm belief that his team members willingly want to do the same. He loves what he does and it is contagious.

"Later I discovered this is typical of Denny Flanagan. If there's a diversion or a delay, he orders enough pizza or McDonald's hamburgers for everybody on the plane. While they eat, he explains in detail why there's a delay and jokes around with them: 'By the way, this is my first flight,' he says. Then, as the passengers make nervous noises, he adds, 'Today.'

"Captain Flanagan raffles off prizes for his passengers. He calls parents of unaccompanied children to let them know their kids have arrived safely. With his phone, he takes photos of pets in the cargo area and shows them to their owners so they will know that their pets are safe and comfortable. He personally helps passengers in wheelchairs board the plane. He distributes his own business cards to frequent fliers with a handwritten note thanking them for flying with him. Nobody requires him to do any of these things. But in true proactive form, he says, 'Every day I work from my heart and choose my attitude.'"[25]

Captain Denny Flanagan knows the tremendous difference between a *leader* and a person who has merely formal authority. Anyone who chooses to can be a leader, and the organization that knows how to help everyone make that choice will have an unbelievable competitive advantage, because an organization full of people like Denny is unstoppable.

MINING THE 7 HABITS

One example of an organization that is successfully turning everyone into a leader is Mexico's MICARE/MIMOSA mining company. Seven days a week, twenty-four hours a day, eight thousand workers in MICARE/MIMOSA's mines grind through coal seams two thousand feet below the surface of the earth.

Established in 1977, MICARE/MIMOSA's only customer is the Mexican Federal Electricity Commission, which buys millions of tons of MICARE/MIMOSA's coal to generate electricity at the nearby José Lopez Portillo electrical plant. From this effort, a full 10 percent of Mexico's electricity needs are met. A few years ago, however, production was beginning to drop even as demand for electricity was rising.

According HR Manager Jorge Carranza Aguirre, "We were going through difficult times. We had to reduce costs while increasing production to meet higher demand. The problem was too much pressure, too much stress on people. Under these conditions, it was each man for himself. There was a lot of conflict between units and between workers and supervisors, and that created slowdowns. We did many good things, but we lacked unity and motivation.

"We had given the workers a lot of technical training and taught them how to operate the machines, but we needed to provide them with different kinds of tools. They needed to be able to manage themselves. When I heard about the 7 Habits, I realized this was the system I was looking for.

"The 7 Habits changed everybody's mindset. At the top, we realized that if we wanted to be a first-world company, we needed a new foundational principle—that people make the organization, and to the degree to which we strengthen the people, we will strengthen the organization. We wanted everyone to be a leader."

As we brought the managers and union leaders together around the 7 Habits, conflict decreased tremendously. Seeing themselves

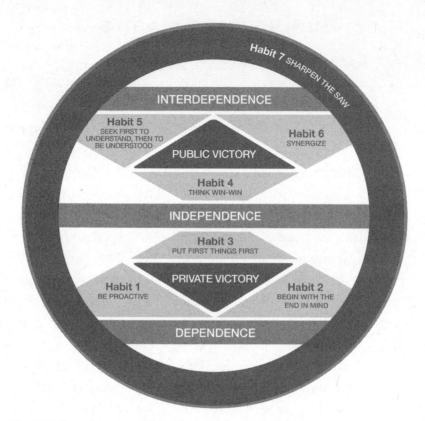

The 7 Habits Operating System

now as responsible leaders instead of victims, miners started taking initiative, setting goals, and collaborating on solutions to their own team and production issues.

Before long, the new culture was spilling over into the homes of the workers. People asked, "What are they doing to my spouse at work!? Now they're coming home, and they want to make win-win agreements, they want to be more proactive, and they have a vision of what they want to do in life—things they never even thought of before." Eventually, entire families joined the 7 Habits classes, and the culture of the community was transformed. When asked what had changed about the MICARE/MIMOSA miners, the wife of one miner replied, "Heart, heart, feeling . . . in every way, in the family and for their coworkers."

Today the 7 Habits are painted on the outside of virtually every building in the mining complex. Miners paste 7 Habits stickers onto their safety helmets before they descend into the mines. MICARE/MIMOSA has captured minds *and* hearts as the 7 Habits became everyone's standard leadership operating system.

ENHANCING A WINNING CULTURE

Centiro is a cloud-based logistics software company headquartered in western Sweden. Their list of clients is impressive and includes iconic brands renowned for supply-chain innovation and effectiveness. Prior to their work with FranklinCovey and the 7 Habits, Centiro had a strong, even admirable culture. They had been designated one of Europe's best places to work, and had a long track record of impressive financial results. CEO Niklas Hedin's challenge wasn't how to fix a broken culture—instead, it was how to take Centiro to the next level of performance. When our colleague, Henry Rawet, first met Niklas to discuss the 7 Habits, he noticed the powerful culture already in place. Together, they determined the 7 Habits could be the catalyst for building on this cultural foundation. Specifically, they saw it as an opportunity to establish the shared and common language necessary to create an enhanced culture of maximum empowerment and of getting people to work to their full potential, with better alignment between strategy and execution.

What makes Centiro's story so interesting is the specific role Niklas took in personally owning the solution, and the fact that every employee regardless of position participated in the workshops. Our work with them began with their leaders. Both Niklas Hedin, the CEO, and Lisbeth Hedin, the Facility Manager, became certified to teach the material to their organization, thus making a very clear statement: "These principles are the foundation for how we behave, on an individual basis and an organizational basis." There is no hiding your behavior when you stand in front of those you lead. Centiro's leaders have consciously become models for the culture they want to create and reinforce. Niklas believes that as the CEO, one of his most critical jobs is to develop and sustain the winning culture.

EVERY CHILD CAN BE A LEADER

Even small children can become leaders. Thousands of schools have adopted the 7 Habits as a way to teach leadership to children. Usually, "student leaders" are a small group of gifted, outgoing kids who are always the class officers, the top athletes, or the leads in the school play. But at one school in North Carolina, *all* students are expected to be leaders. Every child is a leader of something. Organizing books, announcing the lunch menu, collecting homework, greeting guests, dispensing hand sanitizer—these might not seem like "leadership" roles, but leadership starts here. The children learn what it feels like to be responsible. They learn that being a leader means being a contributor.

Most students take huge pride in their responsibilities. Some don't want to miss a day so they can fulfill their leadership roles. As they mature, so do their responsibilities: They take over marking attendance, teaching lessons, leading projects, mentoring other students, even grading homework. Every student can lead something. An autistic boy who struggles to keep track of time does small daily routines in the nurse's office. He is so excited to fill his leadership role that he watches the clock like a hawk and is never late for his job. Another boy with a history of discipline problems is assigned to lead the office staff in doing several tasks once a day. He not only shows up for his "shift" but comes back two or three times a day wanting to know if he can help—and his discipline problems have evaporated.

These children will grow up seeing themselves as leaders no matter what positions they hold in their careers. They will understand the key difference between an office holder and a leader—between *formal* authority and *real* authority. This paradigm has had a profound impact on both academic performance, which has dramatically increased over the time the school has adopted this leadership framework, as well as a marked decrease in discipline issues. At the time of this writing, more than 2,000 schools have followed this model with similar results.

What was the result? Niklas told us, "It has done a couple of things. First, everyone knows why they are part of the organization. We've recently gone through a significant reorganization involving the entire leadership team. As with any change, this stirred the dust a little—after all, change can be unsettling even in the best of cultures. We've even had a couple of folks who have chosen not to be part of the organization as a result. Better now than later. Now people are better aligned. We have a process that has become part of who we are . . . it has 'landed' in the organization. The reorganization was met without a single negative comment. People have moved to their new teams and now can focus their entire energy on executing the strategy, with a new leadership team. We strive to operate in constant synergy."

Niklas' experience matches the advice of John Kotter, legendary Harvard professor of strategy: "The central issue [of leadership] is never strategy, structure, culture, or systems. The core of the matter is always about changing the behavior of people." The way to change their behavior is to change their paradigms—to adopt an effective "leadership operating system"—and no priority is more important for you right now.

PUTTING IT ALL TOGETHER: INSTALLING THE 7 HABITS AS YOUR PERSONAL AND LEADERSHIP OPERATING SYSTEM

An operating system is a set of rules that governs behavior. With a strong operating system like Windows, iOS, or Android working in the background, you can smoothly run many applications, stay connected to the world, and feel secure.

A leadership operating system should do the same. It's the set of rules that governs your behavior as a leader. You should be able to apply it confidently to any challenge or problem. It must allow you to connect to the world and stay relevant. You should have confidence that it works and will not fail you.

All of these standards are met by the 7 Habits. "How do you build leaders?" asks Jim Collins. "You first build character. And that is why I see the 7 Habits as not just about personal effectiveness, but about leadership development."[26] With the 7 Habits as your leadership operating system, you'll be prepared to deal with today's chaotic, unpredictable world and anything it can throw at you. Your connections to the important people in your work and personal life will flourish. And the security of the system is unquestionable because it is founded on principles that are universal and never change.

How do you install the 7 Habits as your personal operating system? Pretty much the same way you'd install an operating system on your computer—by downloading it. Read Stephen R. Covey's classic book. Take the course. Find out how it feels to be more proactive, to have a clear vision for your own life, and to unload a bagful of useless "priorities." Discover what happens when you approach people with a win-win mindset, when you stop trying to "fix" them and just understand them, and when you welcome their unique contribution to your life and work.

> "How do you build leaders? You first build character."
> —JIM COLLINS

If you practice the 7 Habits, you won't need a fancy title to be a leader—you'll become a leader naturally.

Now, how do you help turn other people into leaders? As Gary Hamel asks, "What can we do to help teach people what it means to exercise leadership when they don't have formal authority?"[27] In other words, how do you install the 7 Habits Operating System *into other people*?

Whole teams and organizations have been transformed by getting educated together on the 7 Habits. Some leaders also have actively implemented the 7 Habits as a standard of behavior. Your influence might not extend that far right now. But as you model the 7 Habits in your own work, as the principles bear abundant fruit in your life, people will notice and your influence will inevitably grow. You'll find them following your example—which makes you a leader.

But you can do much more than model the 7 Habits. You can do a mental "download" of the 7 Habits Operating System with your team. Follow the upcoming instructions carefully, and you'll be doing the job you need to do *now*.

THE 7 HABITS OPERATING SYSTEM: INSTRUCTIONS FOR DOWNLOADING

Here are seven commitments you can make right now—today—as you start your personal journey toward becoming a more effective leader who models to others how they can be a highly effective leader as well:

PRINCIPLE	COMMITMENT

1
 	
PROACTIVITY
	Get into the habit of taking initiative. Use proactive language.
	
	Stop saying:
	    "I can't do that, we don't have the resources."
	    "They won't let us."
	    "I'm not responsible."
	
	Say instead:
	    "I can do that."
	    "I can find the resources."
	    "We haven't talked to the right people yet."
	    "I'm responsible for my life and my work—no one else."
	
	What is a situation where I can be more proactive today?

PRINCIPLE	COMMITMENT

2

―

VISION

Get into the habit of knowing the purpose for everything.

Begin everything with this thought: "What's the end in mind here? Why am I/are we doing this?" Do this before you start projects, meetings, conferences, messages, documents—anything you do at work.

> *What's a situation where I need to define my end in mind today?*

Design your future.

How do you see yourself in a year? Five years? Ten years? How do you see your team or organization? What is your real mission? What do you want people to say about you when you're gone? Write these things down.

> *How do I see my personal mission as of today?*

PRINCIPLE	COMMITMENT
3 ― **PRODUCTIVITY**	**Get into the habit of doing only the things that are truly important and dropping those that aren't.** Plan your work weeks so your calendar fills with top priorities instead of secondary priorities. Ask yourself how you will carry out your vision or mission *this week.* *What can I stop doing today?*
4 ― **MUTUAL BENEFIT**	**Get into the habit of thinking about how to benefit other people as well as yourself.** Who can help you carry out your vision or mission? What's in it for them? Make "win-win" agreements with those people in which you spell out the wins for everyone. *Where am I winning at someone else's expense?* *Where is someone else winning at my expense?*

PRINCIPLE	COMMITMENT
5 — **EMPATHY**	**Get into the habit of really listening.** Stop talking. Listen with empathy, which means dropping your own agenda and fully getting into theirs. (This doesn't mean you have to agree with their agenda; just understand it.) Do this with your coworkers, supervisors, and customers. Seek to understand them before giving your views. *Who needs me to listen to them today?*
6 — **SYNERGY**	**Get into the habit of looking for the solution you haven't thought of before.** Stop defending your territory and your "solutions." In problem solving, say to others, "What if we looked for a solution we haven't thought of before? A solution that's better than anything we've come up with yet? What would it look like?" *What situation needs a synergistic solution today?*

PRINCIPLE	COMMITMENT
7 **Continuous Improvement**	**Get into the habit of getting better—physically, mentally, spiritually, and in your relationships.** What can you do to keep up your energy and keep your mind sharp? What do you need to learn to do your job better? What relationships do you need to work on? If you are a dull saw instead of sharp saw, you won't really be a leader at all. *Where do I need to "sharpen the saw" today?*

You can do more formal things to download this mental operating system, including reading the book *The 7 Habits of Highly Effective People*. You can also get assessments and training to implement the 7 Habits more deeply into your team or organization.

We have been influenced by many global leaders who have installed the 7 Habits Operating System with great deliberation and thoughtfulness. They have taught us the importance of a leader's commitment to living the 7 Habits, to modeling them consistently, to installing systems in alignment with the principles, and to coaching performance consistently.

CHAPTER 3

PRACTICE 1: LEAD WITH PURPOSE

"Effort and courage are not enough without purpose and direction."

—JOHN F. KENNEDY

IN MUMBAI, INDIA, A CITY of seventeen million people, fast food has a unique meaning.

Every day, about five thousand "dabbawalas," or "lunchbox people," deliver nearly a quarter-million home-cooked lunches around this vast, tumultuous city—at high speed *and without error!*

Because people who work in the city enjoy a home-cooked lunch, thousands of white-capped dabbawalas pick up the lunches in characteristic stacked lunchboxes, called "dabbas," from nearly a quarter of a million homes in the suburbs between nine and ten in the morning. The mission: to get this specific lunch by lunchtime to a specific person downtown who is hungry for a hot meal. And it arrives every day—at exactly 12:30 P.M.

As Sarah Sturtevant writes in her Marketing Masala blog, "The mission of the dabbawalas is not couched in flowery words like so many other corporate mission statements. Their simple goal is to serve their customers accurately and on time, every time."[1] They also have a unique value proposition: Unlike fast food chains, they bring a fresh, home-cooked lunch right to *you*, no matter where you are.

People with a simple, unique, powerful mission are the most engaged people. "To the moon," said John F. Kennedy. "Insanely great," said Steve Jobs. "There is a place in God's sun for the youth farthest down," said Mary McLeod Bethune, and her mission was to help them reach that place.

> People with a simple, unique, powerful mission are the most engaged people.

Yet the whole notion of "mission" has produced a lot of cynicism. There are two reasons for that: (1) Too many mission statements are meaningless platitudes, and (2) people in the organization don't live up to the mission.

FIND AND ARTICULATE THE VOICE OF THE ORGANIZATION

There's a huge paradox here. A mission statement is supposed to express the passion of the people who are on the mission. Yet contests are held online for the "worst mission statement." People roll their eyes when anyone refers to the company's mission statement. The bronze "mission statement" plaque becomes a target for pigeons. According to Gallup, *70 percent* of US workers are disengaged—unimpressed and uninterested in their company's mission.[2]

Why are most mission statements just back room jokes? Because of the tremendous irony in trying to engage people's passions and talents in a mission they have no passion for and no involvement in.

At the same time, there is nothing more powerful than the passions that drive people. Tap into those, and you create an unstoppable force. If you get people talking about their passions, they go so far overboard you can't get them to stop. But then management boils out all the passion to reduce it to a mediocre mission statement, and that's where cynicism comes from.

Without an engaging mission, the organization has no reason for existing. People in the organization struggle with an existential problem—they don't know what it all means, so they don't much care. There is nothing for them to engage with.

Shawn says, "I was working with a group of leaders from an organization once, and where I noticed that on the wall of their boardroom was a beautifully framed copy of their mission statement. I read it. The words were nice and the sentiment meaningful. With this group of leaders all sitting around the large boardroom table and the framed mission statement just a few feet away, I said, 'On the wall is your beautifully framed mission statement. Don't look at it. Who can tell me what it says?' Crickets. 'Who can tell me the gist of what it says?' Again, crickets. What followed was an interesting discussion on what a mission statement really is and how individuals and organizations bring them to life."

> Without an engaging mission, the organization has no reason for existing.

Seth Godin says, "It's so easy to string together a bunch of platitudes and call them a mission statement. But what happens if you actually have a specific mission?"[3]

Your true mission is discovered, not created—and it takes considerable effort to discover it. It is not a weekend's work. There's a universal quality in a great mission statement—you sense that it really matters to people—yet there's nothing more distinctive, unique, or peculiar. It's generally applicable and unbelievably specific at the same time.

While your true mission will be unique, in broad strokes they all sound something like this:

We are going where no other people can go because no other people are like us. No one else has the unique combination of talent, passion, and conscience that drives us. No one else can make the contribution we can make.

The dabbawalas are like that. They are intensely proud of the service they have given for more than a century, a service no one can duplicate. Other great companies are like that, too. Passion for the mission governs everything they do. According to Mark Zuckerberg, "Facebook was not originally created to be a company. It was built to accomplish a social mission—to make the world more open and connected." The company therefore draws people who have the energy for that mission.

> "Really successful people say no to almost everything."
> —WARREN BUFFETT

A great mission is expressed in negatives: "No one else goes there . . . no one else *can* go there . . . no one else is like us . . . no one else can contribute this. . ." There is absolutely no whisper of "me, too." As Warren Buffett says, "The difference between successful people and really successful people is that really successful people say no to almost everything." When you say no to unimportant things, it allows you to say yes to the truly important things—those that are in alignment with your mission. In fact, the only way to gain time is to work on the critical few.

So call it what you want. If people are allergic to the term "mission statement," call it a mantra or a manifesto or a purpose statement or a passion statement or "the voice of the organization." Whatever you call it, you need it badly. The old paradigm of management is to put a mission statement on the wall and forget about it; the new paradigm of leadership is to help people find their voice—both individually and collectively. If you are not currently in position to take on the mission statement of your entire organization, we strongly recommend that you master identifying the job to be done by your team. As a leader, you're responsible for aligning the job your team does with the greater purpose of the organization.

THE JOB USED TO BE . . .	THE JOB THAT YOU MUST DO NOW . . .
Put a framed mission statement on the wall	Find and articulate the voice of the organization
	Regularly evaluate the "job your team is being hired to do" right now

DESIGNING AN ENGAGING MISSION

How do you design a mission or a sense of purpose that will *engage* everyone?

The mission should be the collective voice of the people in your organization, not just the leader's voice. Of course, as a leader you are not just an opinion pollster—you do your own rigorous thinking and analysis about the mission. But you are not a dictator, either. Everyone should be involved in creating it. The principle of "no involvement, no commitment" clearly applies to the creation of a mission statement. Leaders might "go off to the mountain" to create a vision, but that vision only becomes an organizational mission when people sign up to make it real. If you want everyone to own the mission, to lead with it, they've got to have a say in it. It has to reflect their thinking, it has to express their potential, and it has to appeal to their souls.

> "Voice lies at the nexus of talent . . . passion . . . conscience . . . and need."
> —STEPHEN R. COVEY.

As Stephen R. Covey taught, "The voice of the human spirit—full of hope and intelligence, resilient by nature, boundless in its potential to serve the common good—encompasses the soul of organizations that will survive, thrive, and profoundly impact the future of the world."[4]

How do you find this "voice of the organization"?

Covey explains, "Voice lies at the nexus of *talent* [what we do well], *passion* [what we love to do], *conscience* [what we ought to do], and *need* [what the world will pay us to do]."[5]

> There is a deep, innate, almost inexpressible yearning within each one of us to find our voice in life.

There is a deep, innate, and almost inexpressible yearning within each one of us to find our voice in life. It's wrapped up in our identity and self-respect. It's not just the talent or passion that surges to the fore without external incentives, nor is it just the urgings of conscience—although these are essential to the voice. It's also knowing that we are needed, that the world values the uniqueness in us.

In other words, an engaging organizational voice or mission must appeal to people's passionate interests, leverage their distinctive talents, satisfy the conscience, and meet a compelling market need. It's not easy to fulfill all of these criteria at the same time, but the leader's

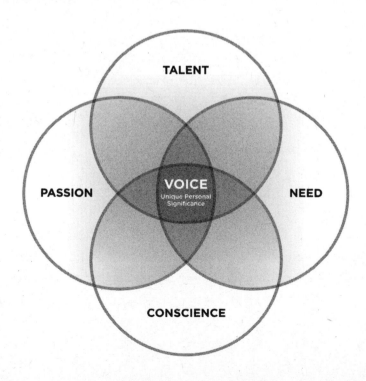

job is to combine all those elements of the organization's "voice." Leaders who do so tap into a miraculous power source.

Begin now to evaluate the mission of your team or organization:

- *Talent.* Are you leveraging the irreplaceable talents of team members? Do you even know what they are?

- *Passion.* Is everyone passionate about their job? Do they come at it with energy and determination, or do they just go through the motions?

- *Conscience.* Are you meeting the demands of conscience? Is your organization doing what it should do? Are you tapping into people's innate desire to be socially responsible?

- *Need.* What is the specific job your internal and external customers are hiring you to do? Have you really answered that question? The job you are being hired to do is very different from a job description. It requires careful stakeholder analysis: What are they trying to achieve through your contribution? What are they willing to *pay* for? Are you in sync with the needs of an ever-evolving market? Are you staying on top of market hot spots, or are they moving away from you?

What you are really doing when you map out your mission statement *is* telling your team story. What anecdotes do you tell about your own successes? Your failures? What is exciting about the job you do? How could you raise the bar on excitement and involvement? Imagine your mission statement as a lead story in the news— what would be the headline? What would make the story viral? It is the job of a leader to engage all stakeholders through a compelling strategic narrative on mission or a team's purpose. In today's world, a leader has a moral imperative to connect the "why" behind the "what" to meaningfully engage their talent. This is most powerfully accomplished by thoughtful and deliberate design.

One organization that has clearly found its voice—and has benefited hugely from doing so—is SAS Institute, the analytics-software giant with nearly forty years of record earnings. SAS has been named repeatedly as America's best place to work; the recognition is now global, as the Great Place to Work Institute has named SAS as the world's best multinational workplace.[6]

"Every aspect of life on the large, leafy SAS campus in Cary, North Carolina, is designed to bring the best out of employees by treating them well," says *The Economist*. The firm provides free health care, sports facilities with an aquatic center, and subsidized child care and restaurants where families eat together. The walls are adorned with a magnificent art collection. But it's not just the benefits that delight SAS people—"it's the challenge of the work."[7] The mission of SAS is to help clients turn the huge volumes of data they now collect into usable intelligence; in other words, SAS people get to find answers to fascinating questions posed by banks, retailers, pharma companies . . . anyone with "Big Data" and a lot of problems to solve.

"If there is a heaven on earth on the job, it is at SAS Institute," says *60 Minutes*. SAS cofounder Jim Goodnight believes that the talent, passion, and conscience of his people make up his ultimate competitive advantage; as a result, engagement levels are high and turnover is extremely low. "Ninety-five percent of my assets drive out the front gate every evening," Goodnight told *60 Minutes*. "It's my job to bring them back."[8]

> "Ninety-five percent of my assets drive out the front gate every evening. It's my job to bring them back."
> —SAS COFOUNDER JIM GOODNIGHT

You can see that the mission of SAS is far more engaging than what you'll find in the vast majority of "corporate mission statements."

SAS engages the talents and passions of its people by valuing those talents and passions *above all else*. It goes far beyond "M&M Wednesdays" and "Free Breakfast Fridays." Clients want innovative business intelligence, so SAS needs the best and most creative people from many fields. The unusual thing they share is that SAS thinks their ideas are actually important! "What makes our organization work are the new ideas that come out of our employees' brains," says Goodnight. As one twenty-eight-year employee observes, "When people are treated as if they're important and truly make a difference, their loyalty and engagement soar."[9]

SAS engages the conscience of its people with a strong commitment to social responsibility. A Corporate Social Responsibility Task Force at SAS integrates efforts across the firm, annually overseeing more than 22,000 hours of employee volunteer work and nearly $20 million in contributions to schools and charities. Senior managers sit on the boards of the World Wildlife Fund and the Environmental Defense Fund. Each year, the company generates from solar sources more than 3,900 megawatt-hours—the equivalent of the electricity used by 54,000 homes for one hour![10]

Again, what about your mission? Are you truly engaging the talent, passion, *and* conscience of people by meeting needs that matter?

GET ALIGNED TO THE MISSION

What's the second reason people are cynical about the company mission statement? The company is so often misaligned with it. The grand pronouncements on the bronze plaque don't line up with the things people are asked to do every day. In short, managers and leaders don't walk the talk. It doesn't matter how fervid the language; if the mission statement is about "valuing customers above all" while management obsesses over everything *but* the customers, people simply disengage from the mission. "If it doesn't matter to the C-suite, why should it matter to me?"

Assuming you really want people to engage with the mission, everything you do needs to align with it. This means carefully examining and (if necessary) redesigning the core processes of the organization— everything from strategy to marketing to R&D to sales to compensation. Are any of these processes undermining the mission?

Every core process needs to support the mission in a simple, visible, and consistent way.

Think of the core process in the dabbawala organization. After collecting the lunchboxes between nine and ten in the morning, the dabbawalas pack them onto trolleys and push them to the railway station. The boxes go by train to a central station for unloading. Each box is color-coded so that those going to similar destinations end up on the same trolley. A given lunchbox might pass through the hands of four different dabbawalas before it arrives at its destination by 12:30 P.M. At the receiving station, the dabbawalas load the boxes onto their trademark silver bicycles. They have only their bicycles, the coded boxes, and the city train system as resources to navigate through one of the largest, most crowded, and most complicated cities in the world.

> Every core process needs to support the mission in a simple, visible, and consistent way.

In the afternoon they reverse the process, picking up the empty boxes and returning them to the residents. That's more than 400,000 nearly mistake-free transactions every single day—for more than a century.

Because the dabbawalas' system of "carrying the curry" is virtually perfect, it has attracted the attention of the Harvard Business School, *The Economist*, the ISO 9000 authority of Australia, and even the Prince of Wales.[11] Scholars and students of supply chain management are amazed. After studying the dabbawalas' system, *Forbes Magazine* writers compared it to a Six Sigma process, which means the lunchbox men make only one error in every sixteen million transactions! How do they do it? As *Forbes* asked, "How can a system based on barefoot men, public trains, and simple, reusable containers" be one of the top core processes in the world?[12]

According to the professionals who evaluated it, the dabbawalas' process works so well because it is *simple, visible,* and *consistent*.

Everyone, from the youngest dabbawala to the chairman of the association, can describe the *simple* process. The dabbawalas know exactly where they are going 100 percent of the time.

The system is *visible*. The lunchbox code contains the entire work process, from start to finish. A few symbols on each lid indicate exactly where the lunchbox came from and where it is going. For example, a box picked up at Vile Parle railway station routes through Churchgate Station—we know this from the symbol of a cross on the lid. Then it moves on to a particular building indicated by blue lettering. The numbers "1–2" communicate the endpoint: the second office on the first floor.

And *consistency* is, of course, the hallmark of the dabbawalas' service. You can count on them without question. The dabbawalas take pride in their consistent quality of service. They wear distinctive white caps and tunics, and their silver bicycles are recognized every where. There is no overreliance on technology, but a lot of reliance on a winning team.

The passion of the dabbawalas means they never let down a customer. When a disastrous monsoon struck Mumbai in 2005, many thousands of people drowned or were lost. The city's massive network of trains, which the dabbawalas depend on, stopped completely. So the dabbawalas left the trains and made their way several kilometers to their checkpoints on foot, carrying the dabbas through the torrential rains and floods. Few if any customers were missed. Uninterrupted service is that important to the dabbawalas.

Of course, as the world changes, the dabbawalas change, too. That's why they are now taking orders by text and expanding their services. For example, their clockwork precision and custom delivery makes them an attractive distribution outlet for everything from time-sensitive software advertisements to investment brochures. As one dabbawala says, "There is a service called FedEx that is similar to ours—but they don't deliver lunch."[13] Through it all, the core process stays simple, transparent, and utterly reliable. Every single day, battling the vast crowds of Mumbai, unbelievable heat, or monsoon floods, the dabbawalas serve their customers with calm consistency.

Organizational psychologist Paul S. Goodman of Carnegie Mellon University observed, "Most of our modern business education is about analytic models, technology, and efficient business practices. The dabbawalas, by contrast, focus more on human and social ingenuity."[14] They focus on the people, on the pride of being unique, and on the strength of commitment to the mission.

What about your core processes? Are they . . .

- Simple?
- Visible?
- Consistent?

What could you do to simplify your processes? Make them more visible? Make them more consistent with the mission of the organization, and consistent in execution?

> People will never engage with a "mission" that is not a mission, that is meaningless corporate-speak.

In the end, people will never engage with a "mission" that is not a mission, that is meaningless corporate-speak. And if they're not asked to live by it, the mission doesn't matter anyway.

But if you want to engage the full power of your people, involve them in finding your organization's voice. Then let that voice govern everything you do.

LEADING WITH PURPOSE: INSTRUCTIONS FOR DOWNLOADING

Here are key steps to lead your team or organization with purpose. Involve your team in discussing these questions. The outcomes should be (1) an *engaging* mission statement and (2) core processes that clearly support that mission.

STEP	DISCUSSION POINTS
1 **FIND THE VOICE OF YOUR TEAM**	• Do we have a written team mission? Are we passionate about our team mission? Does it inspire our energy and determination, or are we just going through the motions? • Does our mission leverage the irreplaceable talents of each team member? Do we even know what those talents are? • Does our mission meet the demands of conscience? Are we doing what we should do? Are we socially responsible? • What is the specific job our customers are hiring us to do? Is it changing? — Who are our most important internal or external customers and stakeholders? — What are their most important goals? — What unique capabilities do we bring to help them meet those goals? What are they "hiring" us to do or provide? • Given our answers to these questions, how can we refine our mission or purpose statement?

STEP	DISCUSSION POINTS
2 —— ALIGN WITH THE MISSION	• What are our core processes? • Do our core processes clearly support the mission? • What do we need to do make our core processes: — Simple? — Visible? — Consistent?

CHAPTER 4

PRACTICE 2: EXECUTE
WITH EXCELLENCE

"A really great talent finds its happiness in execution."
—JOHANN WOLFGANG VON GOETHE

AS A LEADER, YOU MAY have a strong mission that you have communicated well with your team, and you may have a solid strategy for carrying it out. But no matter how visionary you are, you can't truly be a leader unless you produce results. Fulfilling that strategy requires a deeply engaged team—and creating that team is the leader's perennial challenge. Assuming you have an engaging mission and strategy, your next priority is to execute that strategy. Having a great strategy and successfully executing it are two very different things.

How often have leaders announced a great new initiative that dies a slow death? Most strategies fail, not because they are poor strategies but because they are never executed. Jim Huling, former CEO of a major US information technology consultancy and a current managing consultant for FranklinCovey's Execution Practice, says, "You get everybody together in the annual company meeting and announce the strategy for the coming year. Everyone stands and claps and cheers, 'What a great strategy! We can't wait to get on board!' As a leader, that's your best moment. It's also your worst moment, because from that point the strategy starts to collapse. It's not that people don't want to execute, it's that they don't know how—then they start to lose interest, and after a few months, it's 'What strategy?'"

It's discouraging for a team member to get inspired and motivated about a big change—and then nothing changes. In one case, the leaders of a big nonprofit organization, one of the world's largest charities, announced a major change in direction. There was a big event and a showy announcement party complete with banners, bands, balloons, and T-shirts for everyone. Everybody was excited, but they went back to work the next day and didn't hear much about it after that. Occasionally someone would ask, "Whatever happened to that great new program?" They slowly disengaged, but at least they had the T-shirts.

> Most strategies fail, not because they are poor strategies but because they are never executed.

Meanwhile, the leaders wrung their hands and wondered why the new program was failing. They rang up their regional managers, asking them with more and more exasperation to get on with it. The regional managers promised to do so, but then they went back to work and it was forgotten. After a year, the top leaders stopped talking about it altogether—it was too embarrassing.

This scenario might be extreme, but it's more or less like this everywhere. How many carefully designed strategies are slowly gathering dust for lack of execution?

Occasionally there's resistance to a strategy, and sometimes the strategy doesn't fit the market, but by far the most common reason for strategic failure is a lack of organizational focus on the execution of the strategy. Think about it: Leaders give you a new program, a new goal, a new strategy, but your day-to-day work doesn't go away, so you can't give it enough focus. You have to keep doing what you've been doing (remember the mantra "more with less") and meet the new goal, too. You've got to "get back to work." Also, by asking you to do something new, the leaders are asking you to do something you've never done before. They're asking you to change your behavior, which is the hardest thing anyone ever tries to do. Whether you're trying to lose weight, learn the piano, win at golf, or execute a strategic goal with excellence, sustained success requires extraordinary commitment.

> Whether you're trying to lose weight, learn the piano, win at golf, or execute a strategic goal with excellence, sustained success requires extraordinary commitment.

Wharton management professor Lawrence Hrebiniak points out that many MBA-trained managers "know a lot about how to decide on a plan and very little about how to carry it out."[1] So how *do* you get that extraordinary commitment from others? How do you engage them in new and demanding goals when they're already struggling with the whirlwind of the "day job"?

It's no longer enough to have a great strategy. The job to be done now is to get yourself and your team absolutely clear on the wildly important goals, and to discipline yourselves to execute with excellence and precision.

THE JOB USED TO BE . . .	THE JOB THAT YOU MUST DO NOW . . .
To come up with a great strategy	To execute your strategy *with excellence and precision* to achieve required results

THE 4 DISCIPLINES OF EXECUTION™

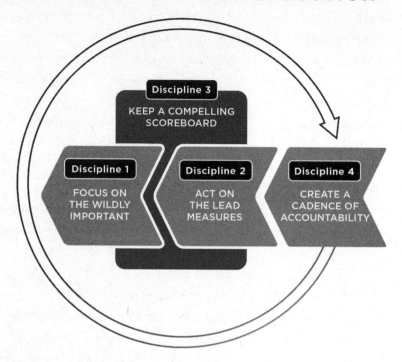

To help you achieve these goals with excellence, apply the 4 Disciplines of Execution:[2]

1. Focus on the Wildly Important
2. Act on the Lead Measures
3. Keep a Compelling Scoreboard
4. Create a Cadence of Accountability

Focus on the Wildly Important

Most people are trying to do too much. To stay engaged with the real priorities, leaders need to carefully distinguish what is important from what is wildly important. A goal that is wildly important is one that must be achieved or nothing else will matter very much. Because human beings have limits, we can usually achieve one goal with excellence, but if we have two goals, it stands to reason we'll do half a job on each. Ask us to reach five, six, or ten goals, and our chances of executing them all with excellence are zero. In investigating the great companies, Jim Collins found that most of them are highly focused on a few key goals: "When you develop your annual priorities, be rigorous about what your top few priorities are—and that should be a very short list . . . Work on one priority, and stop working on something that is of lesser priority."[3]

It sounds obvious, but businesses have a way of piling up "must do" priorities, making it impossible to do a very good job on any of them. One recipe for disengaging people is to overwhelm them with things to do, all of which are "job one" and "top of the list priorities." But if you unleash people to focus on one, two, or three wildly important goals—no more—they will sense the significance of what they're doing and have a chance to win. There is tremendous power in focus. As you prioritize your goals, think about those things that must be done or nothing else matters, focus on those true priorities, and move lower priorities to the back burner.

> A goal that is wildly important is one that must be achieved or nothing else will matter very much.

Be sure to establish a clear and shared understanding of the goal. Leaders often assume the goal is understood by everyone, when in reality there's usually wide and divergent understanding. Lawrence Hrebiniak reports, "I've done consulting where a major strategic thrust has been developed, and a month or two later I go down four or five levels and ask people how they're doing. They haven't even heard of the program."[4]

Shawn reports, "I met once with a group of senior government leaders, the executive team for a newly formed agency with a new mandate. They had already met for days creating their strategic plan, so I did a little experiment: I asked each one separately to tell me the agency's top priorities and key goals. I was fascinated by the response— they were all over the map! Every single one had an extremely different idea of what was wildly important, even though after days of planning they had assumed they were all on the same page."

If a goal is wildly important, it's worth being precise about it. That means you should formulate it in terms of where you are now (X), where you want to be (Y), and by when; in other words, "From X to Y by when." For example, it's not enough to have a goal to "lose weight"—you need to express it as, say, "From 195 lb. to 180 lb. by June 1." Now you have a starting point, an ultimate objective, and a specific target date. It will be easy to tell if you achieve your goal or not.

There is tremendous power in focus.

In 1958, the US space program was significantly behind the Soviet Union's. America's goal was to "maximize our effectiveness in space": nothing specific, nothing measurable, and something of a yawn. Then, on May 5, 1961, in a speech before a joint session of Congress, President John F. Kennedy proposed the goal of "landing a man on the moon and returning him safely to the earth" by the end of the decade. This wildly important goal, "From the earth to the moon and back by 1970," engaged and energized the entire nation. And it was achieved.

If a goal is wildly important and people know it matters most, their engagement goes off the charts—in fact, it's tough to distract them. Formula One racers don't answer their cell phones during the race.

When Tom Weisner became mayor of Aurora, the largest city in Illinois after Chicago, he confronted dozens of important issues. The Fox River district was blighted; the crime rate was sky high; gang violence had reached a high point with twenty-six murders the prior year; scores of businesses had fled the city, leaving an unemployment problem; and the city workers weren't even taking down the annual holiday decorations (this last issue was a sore point with a lot of people). With so much on his plate, Mayor Weisner could have tried to "eat it all," but he didn't. He wisely surveyed his entire team of twelve hundred workers to choose no more than three "wildly important goals." They would decide together what those three were.

Since no one had ever asked them before, the city workers had plenty of ideas. After repeated discussions with them and other civic groups, the city leaders chose three wildly important goals for the year:

1. Reduce shootings by 20 percent.
2. Reduce the resolution time for citizen requests from all city divisions by 20 percent.
3. Revitalize the Fox River Corridor by approving a minimum of 650 new residential units and creating one acre of open space for the corridor.

Everyone agreed that if the first goal was not met, nothing else would matter very much. The image of a dangerous city was destroying everything. The second goal meant a lot to the citizens—to catch up on a huge backlog of requests would rekindle their faith in the city. The third goal was about turning a declining city into a revitalized city. These goals were wildly important to everyone's future, and the people who *set* the goals *owned* them. They were engaged.

Act on Lead Measures

Once you have set clear "wildly important" goals, it's time to define everyone's role in achieving them. Each person must consider, "How do *I* contribute to achieving the goals?" Unless they all know the answer to that question, they will disengage.

In tracking progress on a goal, there are two kinds of measures: lead and lag. The lead measures track actions you set and take to achieve the goal. For example, consuming fewer calories each day and exercising regularly will lead to weight loss (as long as the laws of physics remain in place), so the lead measures are the number of calories consumed and the number of calories burned in exercise each day. The lag measures quantify the results. For example, if your goal is to lose weight, the lag measure is what the scale tells you about your progress. Tracking the lead measures is harder than tracking the lag measures, but you do it if you're serious about your goal: If you do not hit the lead measures, you will most likely not hit the lag measure.

The task is to select a few lead measures that will have the most impact on the lag measure. You could make the mistake of selecting lead measures that make little or no difference. You could give up eating pastries, for example, but if you don't limit your overall calorie intake, that action alone won't matter much. Or you might choose a lead measure you can't control, such as getting the company cafeteria to change its menu. To effectively reach your goals, personally or organizationally, you must choose lead measures you can control and that will make a true difference in the outcome.

As our team worked with Mayor Weisner and his team, it became very clear that cutting the murder rate was top of the list for the city of Aurora. The lead measure city workers adopted was to break up drug gangs by getting the gang leaders off the streets. Within months, the police had swept the city clean of twenty-one gang leaders. As for the third goal, revitalizing the Fox River district would require new, more attractive space for businesses and residents. City leaders set a lead measure to talk with fifty developers about new construction in Aurora—and by the end of the year, they had exceeded their goal and had ninety-five actively interested developers.

How do you decide which lead measures to work on? Here the expertise of the team comes in. The people on the front line probably know more about what actually moves the business than anyone else. The City of Aurora realized that reducing the murder rate was not the sole responsibility of the police force. Other departments could also play a role in achieving this goal. Municipal workers knew that crimes usually happened in poorly lit areas, so their lead measure was to ensure all burned-out city lights were replaced within three hours. They also knew that crimes tended to occur where graffiti had been painted, so they established a "remove graffiti within twenty-four hours" rule as a second lead measure. These are just two examples. Each department created its own lead measures toward the achievement of the ultimate goal.

One international company showed this principle in action as well. Brasilata, a manufacturer of steel containers and one of Brazil's most impressive companies, needed to enact a plan to protect the containers and the contents inside them. Brasilata's industrial-size cans are used all over the world to ship everything from grains to highly volatile chemicals. If their cans were dropped or mishandled, they could be damaged, which, particularly for its chemical-industry clients, could also be dangerous (and expensive, eroding their margins and causing serious legal issues). Building a better, more durable can became a wildly important goal for Brasilata.

Company leaders adopted the lead measure of getting ideas from the workers. They figured the more ideas, the better chance they had of improving the product. Because they engaged the work teams in the issue, the ideas poured in—thousands of them—and one of them really paid off. A worker on the manufacturing line had noticed that late-model automobile bumpers, when hit, will crumple instead of breaking open. When Brasilata applied similar technology to steel cans, the problem was solved, saving the company millions in damages.[5]

The takeaway is to get the team to define the lead measures. Call on their knowledge and their creativity, and watch them get fully engaged. It is critical for them to be involved in the selection of the final lead measure, as they will be responsible and accountable for acting on them—and all will be accountable to these measures.

Thinking back to the weight-loss example, what do you have control over—what you eat and if you exercise, or what number the scale shows? Unless you're manipulating the dial on the scale, it's the former. In the same way, you will disengage your people if you call them constantly on the lag measures—"Why aren't you people hitting your sales quotas?" "Why is the crime rate still going up?" "Why are there still flaws in the product?" That is not leadership. The secret to achieving wildly important goals is *not* to set them and then hope people will somehow get them done. Instead, true leaders work with people to decide what lead measures are in their power and then hold them accountable for acting on those lead measures. People get engaged when they know they can actually make a difference.

Keep a Compelling Scoreboard

Shawn tells this story: "When I lived in Philadelphia, I liked to go down the street to the playground in my inner-city neighborhood and play basketball with the neighbor kids. It was fun to try to match skills. Usually we just fooled around with the ball, but sometimes we kept score. As soon as we started playing for points, something happened on the court: All of a sudden, the intensity level went up. Eyes narrowed, sweat poured, signals flew hard and fast, cooperation increased, and an audience gathered to cheer and groan. As long as we were just playing around, everything was mellow; but when we knew the score, things got serious. *We were engaged.*"

Like the neighborhood basketball players in Philadelphia, people are energized by "the score." Everything changes when you're keeping score, when you know if you're winning or losing. You need a scoreboard so you can tell at a glance how things are going. The people in Aurora got excited when they saw they could "move the needle" on the crime rate scoreboard. As it started dropping, they became more engaged and more creative about moving it even more.

True leaders work with people to decide what lead measures are in their power and then hold them accountable for acting on those lead measures.

That's why it's crucial to keep a compelling scoreboard—a simple picture with only a few numbers on it. "We already have plenty of scoreboards," you say. "We have numbers coming out of our ears." But we're not talking about the vast compilations of data a business runs on. Although those numbers have their place, we're talking about the numbers that are wildly important—the lag and lead measures on the wildly important goals. All we need to see is the lag measure—"Is the murder rate dropping?"—and the lead measure—"How many gang leaders have we cleared off the streets?" These numbers tell us if we're making a difference or not.

FranklinCovey consultants once toured a large aircraft factory where hundreds of workers were divided into small groups, each focused on making one part of an airplane. At each of these workstations, a computer monitor displayed huge amounts of data in tiny fonts. If you really studied these displays—*really* studied them—you could figure out what the numbers meant. We asked the teams why the monitors were there; most of them didn't know, and the ones who did said they never took time to look at them.

> Imagine watching a sporting event on TV, a football match or a basketball game, with every single statistic related to the event displayed on the screen—but no way to see the score!

So we asked the factory managers, "Why all the complicated data displays all over the factory?" They responded, "We want workgroups to be able to see the impact they're making on the production process." They'd missed a key execution principle. Imagine watching a sporting event on TV, a football match or a basketball game, with every single statistic related to the event displayed on the screen—but no way to see the score! That was the situation in the factory.

By contrast, one of our clients, another big manufacturing facility, posts giant scoreboards with just a few enormous numbers showing the company's rate of progress toward the wildly important goals. But that's not all—each shift that comes on can see whether or not they are hitting their lead measures. The plant leader told us, "These are tough union workers. They never come in early and they leave work at the exact second their shift ends. At least that used to be true—until we put up the scoreboards. Now we catch them coming in early and peeking up at the scoreboards to see what the other shifts are doing. When I caught some of them staying late one day, I nearly collapsed. They really care about the numbers on that wall." The scoreboard is essential to engaging people.

The scoreboard is for the team, not just the leaders—that's why it needs to be big and visible and constantly updated. People play differently when they're keeping score. Chris McChesney, FranklinCovey's execution practice leader, sums up the power of the scoreboard: "The highest level of performance always comes from people who are emotionally engaged, and the highest level of engagement comes from knowing the score—that is,

> People play differently when they're keeping score.

knowing whether one is winning or losing. If your team members don't know whether they are winning the game, they are probably on their way to losing."[6]

Obviously, the scoreboard is a simple device, and it gives strategy execution a somewhat game-like quality. But it has a very serious purpose. Professor Hrebiniak reports that fewer than 15 percent of companies routinely track their strategic performance against plan; in other words, hardly anybody's keeping score.[7] Is it any wonder, then, that so many work teams, having no idea what the score is, are profoundly disengaged? The scoreboard enables people to track activities, compare results, and improve performance continuously. By watching the scoreboard closely, they can tell if their lead measures are well chosen. Are the lead measures actually having an effect on the lag measures? If not, it's time to rethink them. By watching the few scores that matter very closely, the team can change strategy if needed. That's what an engaged team does.

So what if you get everyone together and decide on the wildly important goals? You set your measures, you put up your scoreboard . . . and then watch the entire effort fall apart and die.

This could happen, unless you add in the next level of accountability, and here's why: People will be excited at first. They will embrace the new goal because they've helped create it. They will commit to the new behaviors (lead measures) necessary to achieving the goal. The scoreboard will give them focus. But they need momentum to get it going. Unless the team comes together *regularly* and *often* to gauge progress, team members will disengage and wonder what happened to that goal. If you plan to drive from New York to California, you don't just fill your car up once with gas and expect to make it all the way there. You start out making good progress, but eventually you're going to need to fill up again. In the same way, you need to fill your workers' tanks by holding them accountable and reigniting their enthusiasm by showing them how far they've come.

But how do you do that?

Wayne Boss, a professor of management and entrepreneurship at the University of Colorado Boulder, got interested in what he called the "regression effect"—the tendency of work teams to get really enthusiastic about new goals and strategies and then gradually disengage. Boss is a student of team dynamics, so he spent a lot of time watching teams come together, make plans, get fired up, and then forget the whole thing. He had watched companies do everything they could think of to psych up the workers about a new initiative: big parties, loud music, rap videos, giveaway programs, celebrity appearances, clown mascots running through the aisles. Most people enjoyed these events and went away fired up—but their behavior did not change. As Boss puts it, they invariably regressed: "During a two- or three-day intensive team-building activity, people became very enthusiastic about making improvements, but within a few weeks, the spark dwindles, and they regress to old behaviors and performance levels."

> "If your team members don't know whether they are winning the game, they are probably on their way to losing."
> —CHRIS MCCHESNEY, FRANKLINCOVEY

Boss experimented with many ways to keep engagement high, but by far the most effective was to just meet regularly and often to monitor progress. We call it a "cadence of accountability." Cadence is a "balanced, rhythmic flow" of activity, like a cycle that repeats itself.

If your team goal is in fact wildly important, you can't afford not to have a cadence of accountability.

Create a Cadence of Accountability

The cadence of accountability is a simple, four-step process that will help you and your team cut through the clutter and chaos of the day-to-day and engage in your department or organization's wildly important goals.

Here's how the cadence works.

First, make sure everyone on the team can influence the goal. The goal defines the team—don't include people who can't "move the needle" on the scoreboard. In your first meeting, make sure everyone's role in achieving the goal is clearly defined (you might want to do this in a private one-on-one meeting). Practice the first part of Habit 5 ("seek first to understand") as you gather each team member's perspective. Then ask, "What will you contribute?" Then, and only then, practice the second part of Habit 5 ("then to be understood") and give your perspective. Then be synergistic (Habit 6) and forge the best possible solution and agreement.

Boss describes this role negotiation this way: The leader and the team member "clarify their expectations of each other, what they need from each other, and what they will contract to do." Stephen R. Covey calls this contract a "win-win agreement," in which all parties define what their "wins" are.

Next, meet with the whole team at least weekly (after all, we're talking about a wildly important goal) to check progress. If you don't meet for two, three, or more weeks, team members *will* disengage from the goal in the midst of everything else they have to do. This meeting is *not* your staff meeting—its sole purpose is to move the goal forward.

The agenda of the meeting is simple. Start by reviewing the scoreboard. Is the lag measure moving in the right direction? Are the lead measures having any effect? Are we where we're supposed to be, or have we slipped behind? Should we reconsider our lead measures?

Then review the agreements, the things each team member committed to do the prior week. Celebrate successes and help people who are running into barriers. This is the value of a complementary team: If a team member encounters an obstacle, other team members might be able to help remove it. The leader in particular can do things no one else can, such as getting access to resources and talking to executives.

Finally, make new commitments for the next week. What's the one thing each team member can do that will have the most impact on the measures? These commitments are recorded and shared and form the agenda for the next meeting. Keeping your commitments to your team can engage you more than anything else.

After studying hundreds of teams over a decade, Boss found that if these meetings are held on a regular basis (weekly, biweekly, or monthly), and follow the agreed-upon agenda, performance can stay high without regression for several years. "Without exception . . . group effectiveness was maintained only in those teams that employed [the process], while the teams that did not use it evidenced regression in the months after their team-building session."[8]

Boss also found that the cadence of accountability is "most effective when conducted in a climate of high support and trust. Establishing this climate is primarily the responsibility of the [leader]." He explained that leaders must be ready to ask the difficult "why" questions if tasks are not completed, but they must do so with the attitude of helping to "clear the path."

Teams used to this approach become semiautonomous. For example, a similar process is followed by grocery chain Whole Foods Market, where small teams are responsible for their own P&Ls and make their own decisions about improving them. Gary Hamel says,

"They are held accountable for very challenging targets . . . This is not some romantic thing—'Let's just give everybody more power.' Equip them, give them the information, and make them accountable to their peers."[9]

By using the cadence of accountability, you will give your team members the support and feedback they yearn for. More than 60 percent of the nation's employees—especially the twenty-eight-and-under Millennials—say they don't get enough feedback. Many managers give feedback only once a year: at performance appraisal time. That's like a basketball coach telling the players at the beginning of the season, "You're going to go out and play thirty games, and at the end of the season, I'll evaluate your performance." Frequent feedback relates directly to performance.

By following these principles and this process, you will do more to create a highly engaged, self-starting team than anything else you can do.

THE 4 DISCIPLINES AND TEAM ENGAGEMENT

Now, what happened to the city workers in Aurora, Illinois, as they started to live by the principles of excellent execution? The Aurora *Beacon-News* reported that "the city missed its first goal—shootings were reduced by 14.5 percent, rather than 20 percent—but the following two goals were achieved. Only a few departments fell short of the 20 percent reduction in response time, and the two big development agreements for projects on either side of the river exceeded the goal for residential units and open space." Additionally, murders dropped from thirty to two; in the most recent year, no murders at all occurred in the city of Aurora.[10] In this case, the result was not just an improvement in the "numbers." It literally saved lives.

One more story.

For a century and a half, Leighs Paints has rolled out huge drums of the finest, most durable paint in the world. The firm, located near Manchester, England, is the world's largest manufacturer of the heavy-duty paint used on ships, bridges, and oil platforms— structures that must withstand weather and rough use. But over the years, Leighs ran into real trouble in the marketplace—global competition has meant pressure on pricing and a tough market for raw materials. Worst of all, Leighs' entrenched corporate culture wasn't responding well to the intensifying demands of business in the twenty-first century. After several years of decline, the leaders knew the company was facing collapse. "It was that serious," says CEO Dick Frost.

Now, in what can certainly be described as an amazing turn-around, Leighs is in great form again. Revenues are up significantly, market dominance is increasing, and the firm has been acquired by global powerhouse Sherwin-Williams.

What happened? We can understand the results if we look at it through the lens of culture. So what was the culture like before?

"Leighs was an old established business. It was a pointy, command-and-control, don't-think culture," explains Frost, also noting how employees were seldom asked for their opinions, and their contributions were limited to showing up and making paint. Many were completely disengaged emotionally and mentally from the company. "When asked how many people worked at Leighs, the black humor answer was, 'About half of them.'"

Adds Roger Williams, a company director, "Leighs still practiced some of the industrial processes from the 1800s. There was a complete disjointment between what the management thought was going on and what was actually happening. Clients were unhappy with both product and service—nearly six hundred complaints were logged in one year. Employee satisfaction figures were painful. Finally, in the face of growing competition and declining margins, Leighs found itself hamstrung by a command-and-control culture of disengaged employees."

About this time, Dick Frost became CEO of Leighs. An advocate of the 7 Habits and the 4 Disciplines of Execution, Frost introduced some ideas for change. He listened carefully to the workforce, trying to get a sense of the overall health of the culture. The company launched a change process with a new leadership style willing to think win-win, to listen, and to synergize. As they internalized the 4 Disciplines, energetic discussions produced wildly important goals at each level of the company. Line people took a hand in creating the company goals, a shared cadence of accountability was established, and leaders actively began to clear obstacles out of the way. Constancy of purpose developed across divisions of the company. "It used to be a joke," explained Kaizen internal manager Paul Taylor, "that when you walked across the hall from Sales to R&D, you needed to bring a passport." No more.

"The 4 Disciplines were useful to make sure we delivered," explains Leighs HR director Mike Green. "Health Check Scorecards" were posted in every department so everyone could see what progress was being made toward the goals each week. Leaders changed their mindset about their roles—their job was to support the line people, not the other way around. An atmosphere of trust emerged.

> "We probably put more time and effort into the culture aspect than we do into the financial aspects of the business."
> —ROGER WILLIAMS, LEIGHS PAINTS

Dramatic change did not happen overnight, but a few years after launching the new culture, Leighs Paints was showing quantum improvements on every measure that counts: steady gains in revenue, a fourfold decrease in the accident rate, and hundreds of new efficiencies added to the factory floor. "On time, in full" became the mantra for delivering orders, and teams constantly worked at moving that needle. One year, not a single employee grievance was filed. Meanwhile, productivity soared: At the start of the change process, each worker produced

19,466 liters of paint; within eight years that number had gone up to 38,606 liters (about a 100 percent increase); and operating costs had declined 20 percent.

Roger Williams says, "We continue to grow the culture. I think we probably put more time and effort into the culture aspect than we do into the financial aspects of the business. Now there are 262 people at Leighs Paints who turn up every day to do their best efforts for what they get paid to do. They feel the need to do it. We don't have to tell them anything."[11]

Everybody talks about accountability. The word makes people shiver, because it's filled with fear. But the accountability created by the 4 Disciplines of Execution is personal; instead of being accountable for things you can't influence, you're accountable for a commitment you make yourself. The question we as consultants have our clients ultimately answer is, "Did we do what we committed to each other as promised?" When the answer is yes, the client's group feels like a team, grows in respect and trust for one another, and becomes more and more deeply invested in the success of the team. Ultimately, the execution process is about real human engagement. And that engagement brings real results.

EXECUTING WITH EXCELLENCE: INSTRUCTIONS FOR DOWNLOADING

Meet with the team and have the following discussions.

DISCIPLINE	DISCUSSION POINTS
1 **FOCUS ON THE WILDLY IMPORTANT**	• What are our most important goals? • Which of these goals are "wildly important"? (That is, if we don't achieve these goals, nothing else matters much.) • Can we narrow these wildly important goals down to three or fewer? • What is the measure of success on each goal (the lag measure)? Can you write your WIG in the "X to Y by when" format?
2 **ACT ON THE LEAD MEASURES**	• What are the one, two, or three key actions that will drive success on each goal? What do we need to do differently? • How will we measure those actions?
3 **KEEP A COMPELLING SCOREBOARD**	• Who will create a scoreboard with both lag and lead measures? • Who will maintain the scoreboard, updating it regularly and frequently?

4
—
**CREATE A
CADENCE OF
ACCOUNTABILITY**

- What is the scoreboard telling us? Are we moving the lag measure? Are the lead measures influencing the lag measure? Do we need to consider other lead measures?

- What have we learned about the right way to move the scores?

- What commitments did you make the last time we met? How are you doing on your commitments? What can we do to "clear the path" for you, to help you keep your commitments?

- What commitments will you make to "move the needle" this coming week?

CHAPTER 5

PRACTICE 3: UNLEASH PRODUCTIVITY

"If you want to build a ship don't herd people together to collect wood and don't assign them tasks and work, but rather teach them to long for the endless immensity of the sea."

—ANTOINE DE ST. EXUPÉRY

THE GREAT ARCHIMEDES (287–212 B.C.), one of the world's finest mathematicians, was a man before his time. Not only did he pioneer the techniques of what became integral calculus and figure the approximate value of π (pi), but he is also said to be the father of the machine age by discovering and putting to use the properties of levers and pulleys.

In a letter to his friend, King Hieron II of Syracuse, Archimedes said, "Give me a place to stand and I will move the world." The king took him up on this claim and had the largest merchant ship of the age, the *Syracusia*, deliberately beached by a team of thousands of men and horses and fully loaded with cargo. For days they struggled and strained to ground the giant vessel. Then the king challenged Archimedes to move the ship back into the water by himself.

The story goes that Archimedes attached to the ship a complex machine made of levers and pulleys and, sitting at some distance from the port, gently pulled a rope through the machine. To the amazement of the king, the ship moved in a straight line back into the water. By applying the principle of leverage, Archimedes alone did the work of thousands of men.

> **Given enough support, any human being has virtually limitless power.**

Given enough support, any human being has virtually limitless power. Each person in your organization is unique and has an irreplaceable set of gifts, talents, skills, and passions that cannot be found anywhere else. Too many leaders labor under the pernicious paradigm that people are interchangeable, that one worker equals another, that they can easily replace one person with another person. They see a person as an asset, like a computer or a tractor or a robot, easily traded on the market.

It's common in business to speak of people as assets (although they're considered expenses on the income statement), and leaders often toss out the dull cliché that "our people are our most important assets." But people are not assets. An asset is something you *own*—a human being cannot be owned, bought, sold, traded, swapped, exchanged, or returned like a machine.

Too many leaders treat people like machines. You can buy a car, fuel it, wash it occasionally, and take it in once a year for scheduled maintenance to keep it running without much thought. If something goes wrong, you can get it fixed or trade it in for a new one. Often leaders do the same with people: They buy a worker, pay her, and bring her in once a year for a performance review to make sure she is "doing what it takes" to achieve the organization's productivity goals. If something goes wrong, they get her fixed (send her over to HR) or trade her in for a new one. The leader shakes her head, wondering why that employee is not as excited or motivated as she to give a little "extra effort."

The old industrial paradigm that an employee is an interchangeable cog in the machine is the most important reason why people are disengaged in the workplace, refusing to give the "extra effort." That's why the most important job to be done now is to replace that paradigm with a new paradigm: *that every person is uniquely powerful.* Your job as a leader is to unleash that power.

For years now, the mantra of leaders has been "Do more with less"—cut costs, leverage assets, maximize efficiencies—and it's a good paradigm, as everyone knows. The problem is, it isn't sufficient anymore. Some leaders even use that mantra to abuse people, loading more and more work on them without giving them the right kind of support. More often, leaders simply don't understand the principle of leverage. Remember Archimedes: One person has virtually limitless power, given the right mindset, the right tools, and the right place to stand.

THE JOB USED TO BE . . .	THE JOB THAT YOU MUST DO NOW . . .
Do more with less	Unleash and engage people to do infinitely more than you imagined they could.

The new mantra is this: "Unleash people and they will choose to do infinitely more than you ever imagined they could."

In the Industrial Age we leashed people to the ship as Hieron did and instructed them to drag it. It was hard work, but they did it. Today, if you're mentally still stuck with that mindset, you have fewer people leashed to the ship, and you're piling on cargo ("more with less"), so they're getting burned out instead of fired up, exhausted instead of energized. This is not the way to engage them.

The "more with less" trend was going on long before the financial crisis of the twenty-first century, which made things substantially worse. The workforce shrank even further, and those left behind have been taking on more and more excessive workloads, putting real strain on family life and social relationships.

The result is that a third of Americans are now experiencing chronic work stress.[1] According to the *Journal of the American Medical Association,* only 13 percent of Americans in middle age are healthier than their parents were at the same age; doctors say "chronic stress" is the number one reason.[2] And it's not just the older workers who suffer. A vast number of professionals are burning out in their thirties. It's particularly tough for women who have to deal with the "double shift" of work and motherhood.[3]

> In Japan, ten thousand working people die each year from *karoshi,* the Japanese term for "death from overwork."

The problem of burnout is worldwide. In Britain, work-related mental health conditions such as stress, depression, and anxiety cost UK employers about £28.3 billion a year.[4] In India's fast-growing tech sector, "exhaustion and cynicism have increased"[5] and "stress is becoming a huge deterrent to productivity."[6] In Japan, ten thousand working people die each year from *karoshi,* the Japanese term for "death from overwork."[7]

There comes a point where fewer workers trying to do too much simply can't drag the ship any farther, and we seem to be coming to that point. McKinsey & Company has concluded that global productivity is stalling precisely because of an underdeveloped, unleveraged workforce: "To eke out even modest GDP increases, OECD nations must achieve nothing short of Herculean gains in productivity. In the 1970s, the United States could rely on a growing labor force to generate 80 cents of every $1 gain in GDP. During the coming decade

. . . that ratio will invert: labor force gains will contribute less than 30 cents to each additional dollar of economic growth . . . The challenge is even greater in Western Europe, where no growth in the workforce is expected . . . And in Japan, the hurdle is higher still."[8]

That's why your main competitive advantage going forward will be your ability to unleash the latent productivity of people.

UNLEASHING THE POWER OF PEOPLE

Scientists tell us there is enough nuclear energy in a few buckets of seawater to power the entire world for a day—if it could be unleashed. Likewise, there's enough talent, intelligence, capability, and creativity in each of the people in your organization to astound you—if it could be unleashed. Stephen R. Covey said, "Imagine the personal and organizational cost of failing to fully engage the passion, talent, and intelligence of the workforce. It is far greater than you can possibly imagine."

In the Industrial Age, money was the key motivator. Now, financial incentives fall short of engaging people. Salary is a "hygiene factor"—it's expected. So what does motivate them? A monumental Towers Perrin study showed that knowing their contribution is valued means far more to workers than their salary does. No other motivational factor—money, opportunity, trust, or communication—counts as much as appreciation.[9] Knowing that your contribution is meaningful matters more than anything else.

> Knowing their contribution is valued means far more to workers than their salary does.

"The least of things with meaning is worth more in life than the greatest of things without it," said Carl Jung. Almost every worker feels this way, as scholars recently found when surveying people across generations. It doesn't much matter how old we are or the kind of work we do. "We all want the same basic things out of work," concludes Wharton Professor Adam Grant. "Whether we're Boomers, Gen Xers, or Millennials, we're searching for *interesting, meaningful jobs* that challenge and stretch us."[10]

Meaning is the key to engaging people. It's more important than money. It's even more important than happiness. For instance, in describing new research by Barbara Frederickson and her colleagues on two types of happiness—euidaimonic and hedonic—*Nature World News* noted that "even on a molecular level, the human body is able to distinguish between a sense of well-being derived from a profound, 'noble' purpose versus simple self-gratification."[11] Too much "feel-good living" (hedonic) seems to increase inflammation, raise stress levels, and weaken the immune system, whereas "meaningful living" (eudaimonic) is associated with better immune responses and capacity to handle adversity.[12] Meaning is good for you. It's also good for the organization you work for—the more people find their work meaningless, the worse it is for the business.

Some will say, "It's my job to pay them. It's their job to find meaning in what they do." They have the old organizational mindset that Daniel Pink has described: "Humans by their nature seek purpose—to make a contribution and to be part of a cause greater and more enduring than themselves. But traditional businesses have long considered purpose ornamental—a perfectly nice accessory, so long as it didn't get in the way of the important things."[13]

Think about your organization. Have you developed a culture of "busy"?

The other vitally important component to unleashing a person's power is a sense of accomplishment. A person can know his purpose and be passionate about it, but in today's world of "do more with less," where employees are more accessible (thanks to technology) and thus are buried by demands, crises, matrixed teams, and more, he may be left wondering why, at the end of each day, he was so busy but felt so unaccomplished.

Think about your organization. Have you developed a culture of "busy"? Is your culture one where the award goes to the person who stayed latest at night versus the one who executed perfectly on a key project or goal and still left at a reasonable hour? Have you created a culture of "reward for rescue at the eleventh hour," instead of reward for a great root cause analysis that removed a chronic issue and unleashed millions to the bottom line? Have you provided the processes and methods that allow high-impact projects to get completed on time and with high quality, reducing both redundancy and re-work? Have you equipped your people with the communication skills to powerfully and precisely inform and persuade others to action to reduce the disease of unproductive meetings?

Nobody wants to be buried under a load of meaningless busy work, then have to push through to the voluminous number of

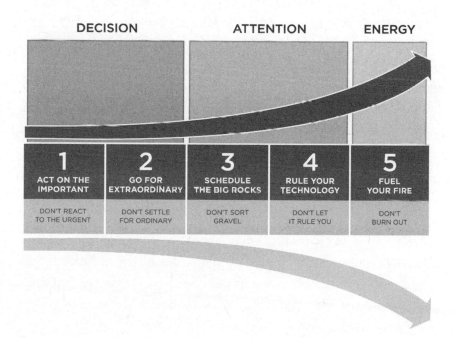

Productivity Choice

deadlines to hit. If the work isn't engaging people, and they are not equipped with the tools to execute with excellence, you need to back up and think seriously about how you expect your people to execute on their best efforts in the Knowledge Worker Age. Your people's greatest assets are their brains, no longer just the hands and backs that the Industrial Age required. We are well out of the Industrial Age, and it's time more leaders come to terms with this. As Peter Drucker said, "The most important contribution management needs to make in the twenty-first century is similarly to increase the productivity of knowledge work and the knowledge worker."[14] So what are the root problems for the knowledge workers of the twenty-first century?

TWENTY-FIRST-CENTURY PRODUCTIVITY BARRIERS

FranklinCovey has been the leader in time management for many years. We've trained more than 25 million people and enabled that learning with our famous Franklin Planner tools. We've helped people manage "time," but today's productivity problems go far deeper than just managing units of time. The Knowledge Worker Age has a few specific challenges that allow the time to just "go by," which can leave us feeling unaccomplished and weary at the end of a day.

Productivity Problem 1: We're Making More Decisions than Ever

Think about it: Every email, demand, request, phone call, and idea is a decision your brain is required to make. During the Industrial Age, workers on an assembly line put one part on one machine a hundred times a day. They had few choices and fewer decisions to make. Decisions they did have to make were simple and of low value. Their tools had one, straightforward use.

As knowledge workers, we no longer stand in an assembly line doing repetitive tasks. We have comparatively unlimited decisions coming at us about what to work on, when, and how ("Do I answer this email? Accept this meeting invitation? Work on this project or that one?"). We do our best to handle decisions as they come in, but the decisions we are required to make are complex and have high value. For example, a salesperson's decisions on how to use her time can mean millions in revenue. We might be constantly busy, but still ask ourselves at the end of the day, "What the heck did I get done?"

> We might be constantly busy, but still ask ourselves at the end of the day, "What the heck did I get done?"

One of our clients told us that her sales organization was overrun with emails, fires to put out, and other demands. They were just too, too busy. When asked what the most important activities were for driving sales, she explained that demonstrations led to the greatest closing rate. Yet even though her teams were fully aware of this, they were so "busy" that those demonstrations were not being chosen as the high-priority activities.

Productivity Problem 2: Our Attention Is Under Unprecedented Attack

The dings, pings, beeps, and buzzes each represent a demand and seem to come at us from everywhere. Thanks to technology, the information explosion is huge, but it is almost incomprehensible how huge. By the end of the twentieth century, the entire sum of information produced since the dawn of civilization was about twelve exabytes, or 10 bytes. We now produce this much information in about four days! And that does not include our personal information. We are all in serious danger of drowning in emails, texts, and tweets! The fact that our brain loves the novelty of those dings and pings, which creates an addiction to technology, doesn't help. Thus the paradox:

Technology makes our lives easier, more effective, and more efficient, but it also distracts us and overburdens us because the unstoppable flow of information is out of control.

Productivity Problem 3: We Suffer from a Personal Energy Crisis

Problems 1 and 2 are wearing us out. We no longer work a standard eight-hour day. Our minds are constantly churning, trying to make high-value decisions, virtually twenty-four hours day. Our mode of life today—constant stress, poor diet, and lack of exercise and sleep—leads to what scientists call "exhaustion syndrome." The rest of us call it burnout. We continually push through each day, postponing the renewal time our bodies and brains need. The mantra is "work like crazy and then crash." And, as we mentioned, we get rewarded for this mindset; it becomes a badge of honor to brag about, "Our team was up till midnight." Do your employees receive emails and texts from you at 10 P.M.? Chances are they are stressed over not knowing whether or not they should be answering them. Are they supposed to "work" at that hour? Do they know what you expect?

Some leaders will shrug these problems off, saying, "This is just the world we have to live in. Deal with it." Other leaders—highly effective leaders—will realize the costs of this and take action.

> The mantra is "work like crazy and then crash."

In an ongoing FranklinCovey survey of more than 350,000 people of all organizational levels from around the world, respondents reported that they felt they were wasting 40 percent of their time.[15] That's almost half their time!

These vast losses don't blatantly show up as expenses on the P&L or as a liability on the balance sheet, yet they are global and pervasive. And most important? Wasting half your time is completely disengaging.

The more you manage these three problems, the more extraordinary you and your teams will be. If we ignore the fact that it is no longer just about "time management," your workforce will continue to feel unaccomplished, feel like they don't serve a purpose, and disengage.

But imagine if they did feel accomplished, they did enjoy coming to work, and knew that every day they were making a great contribution? What would it mean if your teams measurably reported they felt they were working on important things 80 percent or 90 percent of the time instead of 60 percent? What would it mean if most of their time was productive?

How do we capture what a person's mind and heart can produce? By equipping them with twenty-first-century mindsets, skillsets, and toolsets that assist them in feeling highly accomplished every day.

High productivity and team engagement start with you. Are you modeling the right productivity behaviors? Are you intentionally sorting through all the incoming stuff, making the highest-value decisions every day? Are you conscious of how many decisions—with varying levels of urgency—you ask your people to make every day that may cause overload? Do you realize that your people tend to assume you need everything right now?

Are you conscious of how you use your technology, making sure you rule your technology versus letting it rule you? The greatest way to disengage employees is to peek at your smartphone when they come to you asking you for help or just during a casual conversation. Your brain can only do one thing well at a time; if it is trying to process smartphone information, there is no way you can hear or connect with the person trying to get your attention. And if that is your behavior, you have trained your team to do the same.

Are you known as the "inhuman" who works practically twenty-four hours a day with no breaks? Is this a badge of honor? Studies show that pausing, resting, and sleeping increase productivity by 35%. Modeling this behavior is critical. Once your people see you mastering the art of making the highest-value decisions, staying focused on the *humans* instead of just the *technology*, and taking care of your (and their) mental and physical energy, the faster everyone will expand their contribution.

One of our clients needed to make sure their seven hundred sales reps were at peak performance. The leadership team saw that everyone appeared busy, but realized that the sales reps were doing way too much "other" work, and might not be optimizing their sales. They also believed there was a high level of disillusionment and disengagement. After partnering with us, they were elated with the results they achieved. They told us that people are now speaking the same language around "importance and urgency." The team has a clear and consistent vision of success in both their personal and professional roles, and they are beginning to practice work/life balance. Individuals are also doing a great job implementing technology tools for smoother and more efficient workflow. Last, they continue to focus on wellness and brain health to optimize their performance in each of their identified key roles.

A vice president at another firm shared that he was able to eliminate six hours of meetings each week. Imagine his delight in recapturing that time—and imagine the delight and engagement of his team when *they* reclaimed that time!

We were pleased to receive this insight from Stephanie, a new, twenty-four-year-old elementary school teacher, that she had gained about her contribution in life: "As a new teacher, I had a parent tell me that her son was a better person for having known me. Those words had a significant impact on me. I realized that I don't have to be well-known to make a difference. A contribution of this sort cannot be measured in the way the world measures success, but the effects are never-ending. I want to leave that legacy."

You engage individuals by helping them discover the contribution they want to make in their roles. We each have one or more roles to play in the organization's success. Some people sell, some design products, some do marketing, some process or analyze data and financials—some are on matrixed teams, some are mentors or coaches. But we should not be our job descriptions, whether at work or even at home. It is not so much what we do, but the reason behind what we do that motivates us. We create the vision of success for our roles.

What roles do you play? What is your vision of success in your roles? When you determine this, you will rediscover passion and purpose. So will your people. When they discover and write down the purpose in their role (i.e., what they want to be known for in their role), they are identifying the burning contribution they would love to make.

In this way, you get a clear sense of who these people are, what their gifts are, and their philosophies about their work. People are full of passion and realism, and you need to help identify and unleash the power of volunteered productivity from your team.

Take a minute to think about your leadership role. Write a statement that describes the contribution you want to make. Don't just describe what you do now; write down what you *want* to do in your leadership role. In this way you'll tap into your own passion, discovering what really motivates you and how you can create a better world around you.

W. H. Murray, organizer of the 1951 Scottish Himalayan expedition, wrote: "Until one is committed, there is hesitancy, the chance to draw back, always ineffectiveness concerning all acts of initiative and creation. There is one elementary truth, the ignorance of which kills countless ideas and splendid plans; that the moment one definitely commits oneself, then Providence moves too. All sorts of things occur to help one that would never otherwise have occurred. A

> You engage individuals by helping them discover the contribution they want to make in their roles.

whole stream of events issues from the decision raising in one's favor all manner of unforeseen events, meetings and material assistance which no one could have dreamed would have come their way."[16]

It is amazing what happens when you pause from the "busyness" for a moment, reach inside, find your purpose, and make a commitment to your role statement. When your purpose is combined with determined action, you create a sense of momentum that is hard to stop. This is what it means to live by design rather than by default. When people know the vision for success in their roles, it accelerates high value-decision management and focused attention.

You can help others discover their contribution by having this conversation with them:

"Imagine meeting yourself when you leave your current role, whether it's weeks, months, or years from now. Who are you? What contributions have you made? How do you know? Have you made a real difference to the organization? To our clients? How would you define and measure that difference?

"Have you given the best that's in you? Have you brought your best talents, gifts, and creativity to the role? In what ways? Have you felt yourself stretching, growing, learning? How have you grown? What is the most important thing you've learned?"

As people contemplate these questions, they go deep into themselves. They tap into what invigorates them, what is the root of their passion, and both the leader and team member learn how to engage the individual. If you challenge your people in this way, you will be the rarest of leaders—the one who knows how to release the tremendous inner power of your people.

And you *will* be rare. *The Economist* noted in 2006 that, according to McKinsey & Company, "despite the dramatic changes in the way people work, the organizations in which they carry out that work have changed much less than might be expected." It added, quoting

McKinsey, that "today's big companies do very little to enhance the productivity of their professionals."[17] In other words, twenty-first-century organizations are not fit for twenty-first-century workers.

TAPPING UNTOLD ENERGIES

Be the rare leader who turns this situation around. Contemplate the energy, vitality, and optimism of people who are deeply engaged, particularly in this era when our technology leaves us breathless. We are at the edge of the greatest of times. Former San Francisco mayor Gavin Newsom has this insight: "The reality is, people will build cool things for the sake of building cool things. They will expend countless hours and untold energy for the sake of creating something useful or even just fun. There's an excitement out there, a hunger to try new things, to explore the limits of what all these new technologies can do."[18]

But we can still see you shaking your head, saying, "There's so much apathy out there. People have been knocked around and messed with and worked to the bone. I don't know if they would have the energy to 'engage' even if they wanted to." They've been dragging the ship through the mud for so long that their souls are burned out.

"Apathy doesn't actually exist," says Canadian startup genius Dave Meslin. "People do care, but we live in a world that actively discourages engagement by constantly putting obstacles in our way.

"We're missing the most important characteristic of leadership, which is that it comes from within, it means following your own dreams *uninvited*, and then working with others to make your dreams come true. Companies are so uninspiring and uncreative, feeding cynicism at the expense of bold and creative ideas. Of course people are apathetic. It's like running into a brick wall."[19]

The following example illustrates the impact that can come from tapping into passions, even in the face of daunting obstacles. Karen and Bob Hahne were in their forties, with a house full of young children, when they received a call at home one evening. Karen happened to answer the phone. It was social services. The Hahnes had adopted three children years before, so it wasn't entirely unusual to receive a call from social services. The caller told her they had just learned of a baby boy who needed a home; would Karen be interested in adopting another child? "This child was born with Down syndrome. He will have many special challenges and will require unique care," they said.

So the Hahnes started a new adventure with their new son, Reed. Something about him engaged their souls and ignited a fierce outpouring of energy.

As anticipated, Reed presented many challenges. The professionals told them to "love him, but don't expect too much." Others advised to keep Reed out of the school system. He would be figuratively crucified, they were told. Another concerned individual asked them, "How can you do this to your other children?" Their response: "How can we not give them this wonderful opportunity to learn and grow?"

Over the next few years, the Hahnes worked with Reed. As expected, his development was delayed, but progress began and Reed gradually responded to their care. They exposed him to fine music, the theater, and other culturally rich and stimulating experiences. Reed learned to talk, exuding enthusiasm for life. The Hahnes continued to explore every possibility for helping Reed grow in his capabilities. They pursued government and community initiatives, only to learn there were few options. But they decided not to sit and fret about it. Learning of other parents of children with Down syndrome who also struggled for resources and support, they started a small group called "Up With Downs Early Pre-School," which met a couple of days a week in a local high school. There, both children and parents could learn and help each other.

Word began to spread. More and more parents came seeking education and support. Two mothers wrote a grant proposal and, much to their surprise, got it. The program, known as "Kids on the Move," grew beyond those facilities, and it became clear they needed their own building. With little funding and escalating demand, the Hahnes and other parents persevered. They begged for money, got government grants, and enlisted the help of a generous community. Today, Kids on the Move is a substantial school for children from birth to age three, and the program's influence extends well beyond the school and deep into homes and communities. The program currently serves more than fifteen hundred families each year and employes eighty people.

And Reed? This young man, whom "experts" considered a hopeless case, has grown into a wonderful contributor to society. Not only did he learn to talk, he learned to excel. He attended a wonderful high school where he had many friends. For their school "preference" dance, Reed was voted one of the school's "most preferred," and he successfully served on student council his senior year. He went to college and got excellent grades. He is a regular speaker at youth events. He was won awards for advocacy and addressed many national groups. Not bad for a young man who wasn't expected to accomplish anything.

> The secret to productivity is to ignite the passions of your team.

Once ignited, Karen and Bob Hahnes' passion became an amazing productive force. They faced hardship, discouragement, and the occasional dead end, but their perseverance has benefited thousands of lives and brought hope to many families with nowhere else to turn.

Reed was the Hahnes' secret to igniting their passion. Likewise, your secret to productivity is to ignite the passions of your team.

The first step in unleashing people is to engage the passion they innately possess and the legacy they want to leave. You don't have to invite them to have dreams—they already have them. The secret to quantum leaps in productivity is to find that leverage point of meaning that gives life to the human soul.

UNLEASHING PRODUCTIVITY:
INSTRUCTIONS FOR DOWNLOADING

Here are five steps you can take to master making the highest value decisions, staying focused, and having the energy to unleash your own productivity and the productivity of others:

STEP	ACTIONS
1 **ACT ON THE IMPORTANT, DON'T REACT TO THE URGENT.**	Make a list of all the things you do during a typical work week. All of them. Don't forget email inboxes, papers that need attention, social media updates, phone calls to return, people to get back to.

Draw four boxes that look like this. Label the boxes as indicated.

1. Urgent and Important	2. Important, Not Urgent
3. Urgent, Not Important	4. Not Urgent, Not Important

Drop each action item from your list into one of the four boxes as indicated. Then follow these recommendations:

BOX	ACTION ITEMS	RECOMMENDATION
1	Important and urgent things, like putting out fires, taking care of emergencies, meeting close deadlines, etc.	Do them and then analyze how to prevent them in the future. If you are honest, you will see that many of the things in quadrant 1 could have been avoided if you had prepared for them.
2	Important but not urgent things, like planning your time, working on long-term goals, continuous improvement, preventing future crises, reading, and learning.	Focus your best time and energies here. If you do, you will have plenty of time for the things that really matter.
3	Unimportant things that are urgent, like some requests from other people, meetings you've been invited to but don't really need to attend, etc.	Say no when possible to these things. A lot of what people ask you to do might not contribute at all to your top goals and personal priorities—and might even be better handled by someone else.
4	Unimportant things that are not urgent; excessive behavior.	Hold yourself accountable to these things. Don't let relaxation or break time turn into excess and take away from more important outcomes.

When you identified the activities in the four boxes, did you limit your responses to work activities only? Go back and list all the other activities in your personal and family lives as well.

Invite your team to go through this exercise. Ask, "What are we doing in boxes 3 and 4 that we shouldn't be doing at all? What are the things in box 1 that we wouldn't have to do if we did better preparation work? What are the things in box 2 that we should focus on?"

STEP	ACTIONS
2 **GO FOR EXTRAORDINARY; DON'T SETTLE FOR ORDINARY.**	As a leader, your task is to unleash the extraordinary potential of people, but first you need to find out what their potential is. You can discover it by having this conversation: "Imagine meeting yourself when you leave your current role, whether it's weeks, months, or years from now..." • Who are you? How have you changed? • What contributions have you made? How do you know? Have you made a real difference to the organization? To our clients? How would you define and measure that difference? • Have you given the best that's in you? Have you brought your best talents, gifts, and creativity to the role? In what ways? • Have you felt yourself stretching, growing, and learning? How have you grown? What is the most important thing you've learned?

Carry out this experiment for yourself before trying it on others:

- **Identify the few most important roles you play and write them down.** List your work roles and your "outside of work" roles.

- **Write a role statement that describes the extraordinary contribution you want to make in each role**. Take your time. Don't just describe what you do now; write down what you *want* to do in your current role. In this way you'll tap into your own passion, discovering what really motivates you and how you can create a better world around you and feel accomplished at the end of every day.

ROLE	CONTRIBUTION STATEMENT

Do this exercise with team members. Invite people to write down the answers to these questions on their own and then share them with you.

STEP	ACTIONS
3 — SCHEDULE YOUR PRIORITIES, DON'T PRIORITIZE YOUR SCHEDULE.	Each week, look closely at your calendar. Then use the box exercise from step 2 to plan the week. Check off each of the following actions: ❑ Look at your role statements. What one or two key things can you do this week that will have the most impact on your vision of success? These are your box 2 actions. Schedule them. ❑ List all other action items and drop them into the boxes. ❑ Leave box 1 items in your calendar, but ask yourself how you could avoid them in the future. Plan to do so. ❑ Delete or delegate box 3 items. They are not important. ❑ Delete box 4 items. They are not important. Make sure you do NOT delete some relaxation, break, or leisure time. This is most likely a box 2 item.

The biggest threat to your productivity is the very technology designed to accelerate it—your smartphone, your laptop, or your tablet. If you're typical, you might say hello to your tablet first thing in the morning. You're checking your mail, you're reading it during breakfast, then you're playing games, surfing, checking out social media, doing research all day. You're on your smartphone, too, constantly texting, ringing people up, texting again, and texting some more. At night, the last thing you see as you fall asleep is the glow of a screen.

The technology is amazingly useful, but it also distracts us and, even worse, can rule our lives.

STEP	ACTIONS
4 **RULE YOUR TECHNOLOGY; DON'T LET IT RULE YOU.**	Schedule times to check your device to avoid the "constant glance." Stay away from your devices when engaged with people.
	Invite your team to think through their philosophy about technology. How can you use it better? Is your team caught in a web of electronic distractions? How can you eliminate them?

You and your team have a big mission that involves intensive work, so you can't afford to burn out. Keep the fire burning, but in a balanced way. Brain scientists agree that proper exercise, diet, sleep, relaxation, and human connection recharge and even rejuvenate the brain.

STEP	ACTIONS
5 **FUEL YOUR FIRE; DON'T BURN OUT.**	Schedule times to "refuel" yourself. One of your key roles is "self."
	Invite your team to make personal plans to take care of these priorities.

CHAPTER 6

PRACTICE 4: INSPIRE TRUST

"Trust is the highest form of human motivation. It brings out the very best in people."

—STEPHEN M. R. COVEY

I N HIS CLASSIC BOOK *The Speed of Trust,* our friend and colleague Stephen M. R. Covey explained that the first imperative of a leader—at work or at home—is to inspire trust. It's to bring out the best in people by entrusting them with meaningful stewardships, and to create an environment in which high-trust interaction inspires creativity and possibility.

Given this, maybe no other job of a highly effective leader is more pressing than to inspire trust in those he or she is leading.

The opposite can have dire consequences. Loss of trust is arguably the main reason we are stuck in a dreary economy. The repeated financial shocks of the twenty-first century have produced steep declines in public trust in bedrock institutions like big business, banking, and government. Many have lost faith in the foundations of society.

Only 10 percent of workers trust their bosses to do the right thing, and only 14 percent believe their company's leaders are ethical and honest.[1] Less than a fifth of the general public trusts business leaders to be ethical and honest.[2] Only 16 percent of Americans trust large corporations.[3] And 82 percent of workers believe that their senior leaders help themselves at the organization's expense.[4] They look at their leaders and see too much self-interest, short-term focus, and ego-driven decision-making.

> Eighty-two percent of workers believe that their senior leaders help themselves at the organization's expense.

Oxford University professor Colin Mayer diagnoses the situation this way: "The loss of trust in the corporation reflects a belief that it exists simply to make money for its owners, its shareholders, and it will do whatever it takes to achieve this. From our point of view as customers, employees, and communities, we are therefore pawns in a game in which we are manipulated for the benefit of others. The repeated recurrence of scandals only serves to reinforce the belief that the corporation is inherently untrustworthy."[5]

Widespread mistrust acts like a brake on the economy. Everything in the supply chain slows down because transactions have to be regulated, verified, documented, and double-checked. Deals take forever because due diligence is now *intense* diligence. Costs go up at every point. An example: The Sarbanes-Oxley regulations in response to the scandals at Enron and WorldCom are unbelievably time-consuming and expensive—one study pegged the costs of implementing just one section of the law at $35 billion!

TRUST—A PERFORMANCE MULTIPLIER

For companies known for being trusted, the bad news is good news. People are hungrier than ever to do business with people they can trust. A Watson Wyatt study found that high-trust organizations outperform low-trust organizations in total return to shareholders by threefold.[6] What's behind the "economics of trust" that make such superior returns possible? Consider this: Trust always affects two measurable outcomes—speed and cost. When trust goes down, speed goes down and cost goes up. This creates a *trust tax*. When trust goes up, speed goes up and cost goes down. This creates a *trust dividend*. It's that simple, real, and predictable.

How do you feel about relationships where trust is high? How effective is your communication with a person you trust? In our experience, it's easy, simple, and fast. Even if we're dealing with a tough issue, it can be resolved quickly with the person. In high-trust relationships, you can misspeak, but you don't feel like you're walking on eggshells, worrying that you'll offend the other person or make a commitment by accident.

Conversely, when trust is low, it seems that no matter what you say, your words are taken wrong or out of context. Communication is nearly impossible, even about the most trivial things.

Shawn tells this story: "During a casual conversation, a colleague once made an offhand promise to me. Over time, things changed and it looked like it would be impossible for him to keep his promise—it wasn't his fault, it was just circumstances. So I was surprised one day when he called to tell me he had finished the work he'd promised to do. Now, this effort came at great personal sacrifice for him, but he'd made a commitment and he was determined to follow through. I had always trusted him, but that day I gained an even deeper and more profound appreciation for his integrity and knew that he could be trusted no matter what. Over the years, he and I have had tough talks about important strategic issues, but our communication has always been quick and easy.

"In contrast, I once had another colleague whose relationship with me was dicey, always clouded by ulterior motives and hidden agendas. Even simple conversations with him were difficult, as nearly every word I said aroused suspicion and offense. It was exhausting, like a slow-motion wrestling match."

Trust is the great accelerator. Where trust is high, everything is faster and less complicated, and where trust is low, everything is slower, costlier, and encumbered with suspicion.

Once we understand the hard-edged, measurable economics of trust, it's like putting on a new pair of glasses. Everywhere we look, we can see quantifiable impact. If we have a low-trust organization, we're paying a tax. While these taxes may not conveniently show up on the income statement as "trust taxes," they're still there, disguised as other problems. Once we know where and what to look for, we see low-trust organizational taxes everywhere, including the following: redundancy, bureaucracy, politics, disengagement, turnover, churn, and fraud. Just as the taxes created by low trust are significant, so the dividends of high trust are also incredibly high.

When trust is high, the dividend we receive is a *performance multiplier*, elevating and improving every dimension of the organization. Specific dividends include the following: increased value, accelerated growth, enhanced innovation, improved collaboration, stronger partnering, higher engagement, better execution, and heightened loyalty. When you add up all the dividends of high trust—and you put those on top of the fact that high trust decreases or eliminates all the taxes as well—is there any doubt that there is a significant, direct, measurable, and indisputable connection among high trust, high speed, low cost, and increased value? Indeed, trust is the one thing that changes everything!

> Trust is the great accelerator. Where trust is high, everything is faster and less complicated, and where trust is low, everything is slower, costlier, and encumbered with suspicion.

In an organization, trust is critical both internally and externally. In fact, given the performance-multiplier effect of high trust, leaders who used to campaign to be the "provider of choice" in their markets should now campaign to become the *most trusted* provider; those who make building trust a priority are obviously going to have a strategic advantage.

At one time, Sue was a key executive in the McDonald's Corporation and met often with Ray Kroc, its founder. She reports, "There were times when Ray could not pay his suppliers within the usual thirty-day window. Cash flow was always an issue in the early years of building the Golden Arches into a global brand. So Ray sat down with his key suppliers, like Coca-Cola, and explained that he may sometimes be late with a payment. However, he promised he would always pay—and he did.

"The abundant response from Coca-Cola deepened his loyalty to the extent that he promised them he would never change soft drink providers. They shook hands on it and to this date, McDonald's remains a Coca-Cola company. I learned about this personally when I was driving with Ray and he found a competing soft drink in my car. He explained his handshake deal with Coke and how amazingly helpful they had been when he was struggling to keep the McDonald's mission and vision alive.

"He then asked why I could buy something other than Coke. When I explained that I enjoyed a sweeter taste, he smiled and said I must have screwed-up taste buds. He was loyal to a fault. Not long after, a Coca-Cola truck pulled up in front of my walk-up Chicago apartment to deliver a year's supply of European Coke with multiple bows and a big card from Ray that read, 'No excuses, Sue—ask for more when you need it. The European formula is sweeter than the US formula. We are loyal to our partners and I am loyal to you. Ray.'

"I learned so much from Ray and all of my great teachers, leaders, and colleagues at McDonald's—more than anything, the power of extending trust. By trusting Ray Kroc, Coca-Cola gained its largest and most profitable customer forever."

Inspiring trust and extending trust—these are often the keys to gaining an unbeatable competitive advantage. And creating such trust is a skill—a performance multiplier—and arguably the key leadership competency needed in today's low-trust economic environment.

THE JOB USED TO BE . . .	THE JOB THAT YOU MUST DO NOW . . .
To become the provider/employer of choice in your industry	To become the *most trusted* provider/employer in your industry

HOW TO BUILD IT: THE FIVE WAVES OF TRUST

But how do you do it? What is the methodology for building trust?

In *The Speed of Trust*, Stephen M. R. Covey presents a "framework, language, and process" that enables us to establish and grow trust at five levels, or contexts, what he calls "The Five Waves of Trust." This model derives from the "ripple effect" metaphor that graphically illustrates the interdependent nature of trust and how it flows from the inside out, starting with each of us. It also gives us a framework so we can think about trust, a language so we can talk about trust, and a process so we can do something about actually creating trust. The underlying principle behind the first wave, Self Trust, is *credibility*. The key principle behind the second wave, Relationship Trust,

The Five Waves of Trust

is *behavior*. The key principle behind the third wave, Organizational Trust, is *alignment*. The underlying principle of the fourth wave, Market Trust, is *reputation*. And the principle underlying the fifth wave, Societal Trust, is *contribution*. While the principles are cumulative as we move from the inside out, creating an exponential effect in growing trust, the first two principles—credibility and behavior—represent the twin building blocks for how trust is built.

Trust Starts with Who You Are

Where does it start? Ultimately, trust starts with you—with your personal credibility. In *The Speed of Trust,* Stephen M. R. Covey explains how credibility is the foundation on which all trust is built, and how, in the long run, you'll never have more trust than you have credibility. Credibility is a function of two things: your character (who you are—your integrity and intent) and your competence (what you can do—your capabilities and results). Competence is visible above the surface, while your character, like the roots of a tree, lies beneath the surface and feeds your success—or your lack of it.

If we were doing business with you, and you knew that we had all the right professional qualifications and skills but didn't keep our word, you wouldn't trust us and everything would stop. Our lack of character would prevent you from doing business with us, even though we might be the best at what we do. Think of the many high-profile athletes and executives with world-class competence whom the public no longer trusts because of some very steep lapses in character.

Conversely, if we were doing business with you, and you knew that we were honest and cared about you, but that we didn't have the right capabilities, were no longer relevant, and didn't have a track record of results, you also wouldn't trust us and everything would stop. Our lack of competence would undermine the trust, even though we might be extremely honest and caring. You might trust us to watch your home if you went on vacation, but you wouldn't trust us on a key project or deliverable if we didn't have a track record of results.

Both character and competence are vital to building trust, with character being the deeper root, the first among equals. Drilling a level down on the character and competence dimensions enables you to assess yourself against what Stephen M.R. Covey calls "The 4 Cores of Credibility"—the first two cores belonging to character, and the second two belonging to competence.

The first core of credibility is *integrity*. To use the metaphor of the tree, integrity is the root. It means honesty, truthfulness, and congruence. It means doing the right thing and sticking to your word. A great educator, Dr. Karl G. Maeser, described in a penetrating way what it means to have integrity: "Place me behind prison walls—walls of stone ever so high, ever so thick, reaching ever so far into the ground—there is a possibility that in some way or another I may escape. But stand me on the floor and draw a chalk line around me and have me give my word of honor never to cross it. Can I get out of the circle? No. Never! I'd die first."[7]

> The motive that best builds credibility and trust is when you care about the people that you're leading—and they know you care about them.

The second core of credibility is *intent*. In our tree metaphor, it's the trunk—part of it is beneath the surface, part of it is above. Intent refers to our motive and agenda. The motive that best builds credibility and trust is when you care about the people that you're leading—and they know you care about them. The agenda that best builds credibility and trust is when you are open and seek mutual benefit—that's called win-win. Think about it: When you suspect someone has a hidden agenda, you question everything they say and do. Gandhi put it this way: "The moment there is suspicion about a person's motives, everything he does becomes tainted."

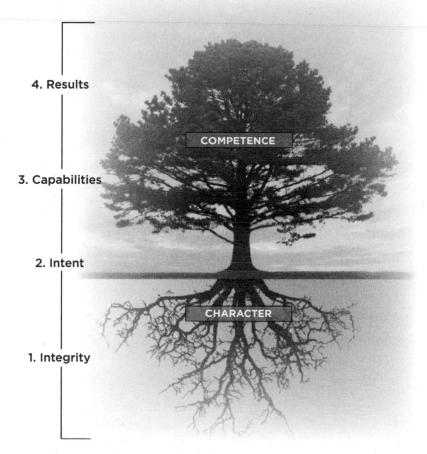

4. Results

COMPETENCE

3. Capabilities

2. Intent

CHARACTER

1. Integrity

The 4 Cores of Credibility

The third core of credibility is *capabilities*. On our tree, capa-bilities are the branches that produce the fruits. Capabilities refer to your ability to inspire confidence, the means you use to produce results. Capabilities comprise your talents, skills, expertise, and knowledge. The key question here is this: Are you relevant? A fam-ily doctor might have integrity, his motives might be good, and his track record might be strong, but unless he's trained and skilled to perform a particular task at hand—brain surgery, for example—he'll be lacking in credibility.

The fourth core of credibility is *results*. Results refer to your track record, your performance, your getting the right things done. Results matter enormously to your credibility. As Jack Welch said, having results is like having "performance chits" on the table. They give you clout. They classify you as a producer, a performer. Results are what convert the cynics. Returning again to the metaphor of the tree, results are the fruits—the tangible, measurable, end purpose and product of the roots, trunk, and branches.

> Results are what convert the cynics.

Each of these four cores—integrity, intent, capabilities, and results—is vital to personal and organizational credibility, and credibility is the foundation on which all trust is built.

Trust Is Strengthened by How You Act

After credibility, the other key building block to trust is *behavior*. Behavior means what you do—and how you do it. People not only judge your results, they also judge how you achieved them—and how you behave in the marketplace. The astonishing spectacle of high-level business and government leaders pointing fingers and fighting each other during the Great Recession probably destroyed trust as much as anything. "In the midst of the worst economic crisis in decades, people saw their leaders not leading but squabbling and name-calling," complains former San Francisco mayor Gavin Newsom.[8]

It's not enough just to talk about a behavior—you have to put it into action, into practice. Think about trust and your relationships in terms of a bank account—making deposits and withdrawals. Deposits and withdrawals ultimately manifest themselves as behaviors. *The Speed of Trust* specifically identifies thirteen high-leveraged, trust-creating behaviors. These include keeping commitments, righting wrongs, practicing accountability, demonstrating respect, listening first, and talking straight. The opposites of these thirteen behaviors diminish or even destroy trust: these include breaking commitments, denying wrongs, shirking responsibility, showing disrespect, failing to listen, and lying.

While the behaviors and their opposites are straightforward and common sense, all too often they are not common practice. The common practice for far too many people and organizations tends to be what are called *counterfeit behaviors,* like "spinning" a story instead of telling it straight, so it is technically true but leaves a false impression. Other common counterfeit behaviors include covering up a mistake instead of righting the wrong, having hidden agendas instead of creating transparency, blaming others instead of practicing accountability, and overpromising and underdelivering instead of keeping commitments. More often than not, it's the thirteen counterfeit behaviors, perhaps more than the thirteen opposite behaviors, that trip up people and organizations, causing them to lose trust. This is because it's fairly obvious the opposite behavior will destroy trust (e.g., lying), while the counterfeit behavior, like counterfeit money, is deceptive— it appears to work but ultimately diminishes the trust (e.g., spinning).

BUILDING TRUST AT FRITO-LAY

While studying and applying Stephen M. R. Covey's work on the speed of trust, the executives of Frito-Lay became fascinated with the idea that building trust could speed things up and lower costs. "Frito-Lay was never a low-trust company," Covey says, but CEO Al Carey wanted to reignite the corporate culture. Like all good leaders, he wanted things to be cheaper, faster, and better, but he also wanted to energize people, to help them "lean into" their work—in short, to reengage them.

Hundreds of bureaucratic rules and procedures were swept away. Layers of decision making were removed. The administrative changes were fueled by the introspective work people did on themselves as they learned a methodology for building trust.

"We didn't just teach skills—we changed the culture," says Cheryl Cerminara, a vice president at Frito-Lay. "Pick two people. One you trust in both competency and character. The other you expect to flub up and/or stab you in the back. Then think about the extra work, energy, and frustration the untrustworthy person causes. Low trust is exhausting and stressful. You hear people say, 'I have to send a million follow-up emails.' 'I worry about it all the way home.' 'It upsets my work/life balance.' Everybody has been in a situation like this. It becomes much harder not to act with integrity when everyone around you is."[9]

The methodology cascaded through the organization and transformed Frito-Lay. For the first time they critiqued their untrustworthy behaviors. They held regular "Trust Talks" at every level, identifying and winnowing out problems. They held checkpoint meetings quarterly to evaluate their progress in becoming a more trusted company. "We learned to trust each other," says Al Carey. "So there was no need for the extra bureaucracy."

In 2008, the company faced gigantic challenges—a sudden spike in fuel prices and the worst economic collapse in seventy years. Then the cost of their raw material—potatoes—went up tenfold because heavy rains spoiled the crops. Financial disaster threatened. But Frito-Lay was ready with a new perspective and a new skillset. With their highly accelerated decision-making processes, they navigated through the threat. The entire pricing system was reengineered in five weeks instead of the sixteen weeks it normally took. "What would normally take us two months of wrangling, we did in ten days," says Carey.

Instead of suffering financial disaster, Frito-Lay shot past expectations and produced one of its best years ever. "It was the best profit growth we'd had in ten years," Al Carey says. "I credit the Speed of Trust process. We moved through decisions that are enormously complex at breakneck speed. We made five sets of tough decisions throughout the whole year, and we never before would have been able to make those decisions as quickly as we did . . . It's the most exciting culture change I've seen in my twenty-eight years with the company."[10]

As a leader, your influence counts. By building up your own credibility and then behaving in ways that establish trust, you'll go a long way toward inspiring high-trust behavior transformations in others.

BUILDING TRUST:
INSTRUCTIONS FOR DOWNLOADING

Here's how to build trust with others[11]:

STEP	CHECKPOINTS
1 **THE 4 CORES OF CREDIBILITY: ASSESS YOUR CHARACTER**	**Integrity** How do you view your own actions? Are they aligned to your own deepest values?
	Intent What's your agenda? Is it hidden or out in the open?

STEP	CHECKPOINTS
2 — **THE 4 CORES OF CREDIBILITY: ASSESS YOUR COMPETENCE**	**Capabilities** Can you deliver what you promise? Are you still relevant?
	Results What's your track record?
3 — **PRACTICE THE 13 TRUST BEHAVIORS**	1. **Talk straight.** Are you honest? Do you tell the truth? 2. **Demonstrate respect.** Do you genuinely care about the people around you? 3. **Create transparency.** Do you tell the truth in a way people can verify for themselves? 4. **Right wrongs.** Do you apologize quickly? Do you make restitution where possible? 5. **Show loyalty.** Do you give credit to others? Do you badmouth people behind their backs? 6. **Deliver results.** Do you get the right things done? 7. **Get better.** Are you a constant learner? 8. **Confront reality.** Do you address the tough stuff directly? 9. **Clarify expectations.** Do you write them down? Do you discuss them? Do you violate them?

PRACTICE THE 13 TRUST BEHAVIORS (*CONTINUED*)	10. **Practice accountability.** Do you take responsibility for results, good *and* bad? 11. **Listen first.** Do you assume that you know what others think and feel without listening? 12. **Keep commitments.** Do you attempt to spin your way out of a commitment you've broken? 13. **Extend trust.** Do you trust others based on the situation, the risk, and credibility of the people involved—but err on the side of trust?

ACTION PLAN

About the 13 Trust Behaviors:

Which of these behaviors are strengths for you?

Which ones do you need to work on?

What will you do about them?

Consider the key relationships in your life:

What are you doing that is potentially eroding trust?

What will you do to improve the level of trust?

CHAPTER 7

PRACTICE 5: BUILD A LEGACY
OF SALES LEADERSHIP

"Talent wins games, but teamwork and intelligence wins championships."

—MICHAEL JORDAN

W E'VE SAID THAT EFFECTIVE LEADERS are trustworthy people with high purpose, who in turn inspire a level of trust that creates deep loyalty among employees, customers, and extended communities of all kinds. Perhaps nowhere does purposeful, inspiring leadership have the ability to bring about more radical transformation today than in the realm of the sales organization. The assumption throughout the past century was that if you wanted greater sales, all you needed was great salespeople, but that's no longer true. Customers' demands are too high, and the selling environment is too complex. Leaders who are in tune with the current reality recognize that building an enduring legacy of success doesn't come from creating great sales*people,* it comes from creating a superior sales *culture*—in other words, what your sales-people do every day.

It's more than a shift of focus within the organization. It's part of a fundamental paradigm shift that corresponds with a host of changes in the buyer-seller relationship. In the past decade, selling has changed more rapidly than in all five decades before. Buyers now know more than ever about their needs and choices, and your competition. They engage sellers later in the buying cycle, after needs, budgets, and options have been identified. Buyers will meet with sellers, but only when the seller has a high-value perspective, point of view, service, or product. And they will no longer tolerate the Twenty Questions game.

On the other side of the table, sellers have tremendous access to data about customers and potential customers, and can easily identify their targets. But sellers are behind the curve, reacting to change with buyers rather than leading that change. Companies are in the position of having way too many demands on their budgets for all the tools, systems, approaches, and training in which they could invest for their sales force. Our research shows that somewhere north of 50 percent of customer loyalty is established *before* customers experience a service or take delivery of a product. This means that *how* you sell matters way more than *what* you sell. It means that the buying and selling experience is a big part of your brand. The leader who creates a sales culture that reflects this understanding can lead an organization to victory.

> Somewhere north of 50 percent of customer loyalty is established *before* customers experience a service or take delivery of a product ... *How* you sell matters way more than what you sell.

What kind of buying experience is your sales team creating? Is it the tired solution-seller/problem-solving model, where they ask question after question with nothing to add? Or how about the pesky pushers, chasing quotas and prodding or even insulting customers?

Or just another seller, who could work for you or any of your competitors, and no one would know the difference? How about the fulfiller? All they want to know is, "How can I help you today?" They aren't able to add real value beyond simply filling orders.

Instead, what if your sellers were well-informed, insightful, trustworthy businesspeople, who were looking to *create value* with and for clients? A sales force like this runs on a combination of critical communication skills coupled with disciplined business thinking and focused execution. This enables your salespeople to talk honestly and put insightful thinking on the table, explore important issues, and collaborate to craft solutions that exactly meet clients' needs. The goal is to help clients succeed.

This model of selling engages and motivates your entire sales culture, empowering the sales force to do something *for* clients rather than *to* them, and unleashes extraordinarily productive behaviors that can lead to unprecedented success. When your organization is equipped with a strong and authentic sales culture, it can move the world. You not only can create better business and better relationships, but also compete more effectively.

CREATING A GREAT SALES CULTURE

The difference between creating great sales*people* and creating a great sales *culture* is well illustrated in the remarkable story of nine young athletes from the state of Washington who rowed their way to victory in the 1936 Summer Olympics in Germany. The young men of the University of Washington crew team had rowed together for less than five months before the start of that year's games in Berlin, and unlike their competitors—many of whom came from elite and privileged backgrounds—the Washington crew was composed of kids from middle- and working-class families, the sons of shipyard workers, lumberjacks, and farmers.

But they didn't need wealth or privilege to win the race. They needed synergy. By literally pulling together and operating in near-perfect synchronization under the effective direction of their coach, the crewmates of the *Husky Clipper* challenged and beat the greatest teams in the world. One of rowing's finest achievements wasn't the work of a dream team of superstars, but "an improbable assemblage"[1] of earnest, committed, and hard-working team members. Individually, they were talented, but together they were unbeatable.

> You don't need sales superstars. You need a super sales culture, where ordinary people do extraordinary things.

The truth is, you don't need sales superstars. You need a super sales culture, where ordinary people do extraordinary things. Unfortunately, our hands-on research has shown that business leaders tend to think about maintaining the culture of their sales organization in the same way that the Mississippi River floods the delta. Every seven years, this force comes along and destroys everything in its wake. It replenishes the soil, and then the nourishment is depleted over time until the flood returns. This approach is never going to create a sustainable, best-in-class sales culture and organizational sales capability.

Imagine if a software developer said, "Once our people learn a certain way to code, we're never going to give them any more education or information." How long would it be until they were irrelevant in the computing space and their people unemployable? A year? Maybe three? They'd be out of business. And yet companies routinely treat their sales teams this way.

If what you're trying to build is a sales legacy, then that goal requires ongoing care and feeding. Unfortunately, there's a common belief that building a high-performance sales culture and capability is both difficult and expensive. But it doesn't have to be hard, and it only costs too much if you try to do too much. The truth is that instead of spending like the seven-year flood, the whole process can be better served by smoothing out the economic curve. Rather than investing enormous amounts of money in sales performance improvement one year, followed by a multiyear drought, your organization can commit a smaller amount every year to engage in a powerful, renewable cycle in which you define and focus on a target, measure results so that you can fine-tune, and continuously improve. By doing this, you can actually *avoid* going through a hard and expensive process.

There are leaders in industries who see the value of this approach and have the courage to stand up for it, saying, "This is how we're going to run. This is what it means to be part of this community." Our Sales Performance Practice Leader, Randy Illig, speaks with admiration about one client of ours, a chief sales officer, who was recruited to join an ailing company that, despite twenty years in business and multibillion-dollar sales, had lost its way. Among other troubles, the organization was experiencing extensive turnover in the executive ranks, and the sales force was fractured, with one sales force for each of the five operating units. "There was nothing consistent in how they worked with customers or how they thought about selling," Randy says. "The sales organization was a group of individuals who sold. It wasn't an organization with its own heartbeat or positive sales culture."

The new sales leader decided that what the company actually needed wasn't new or more salespeople; in fact, he eliminated a large number of the team. Rather, they needed to figure out how to become a great selling organization, and how to create a culture of high performance around selling. Over the course of three years, working with FranklinCovey's Sales Performance Practice, this sales leader took a company where revenue was shrinking, performance was low and getting worse—and where there was tremendous turnover and a lack of consistency in the sales force and sales management ranks—and created a unified sales culture for the first time in the company's twenty-year history.

To do it, he consolidated the group into one selling organization and gave the individuals an identity, both in name and purpose. He instituted all the things that you'd see in any great culture. He made performance expectations and processes clear. He invested in education and tools. He aligned salespeople's compensation more clearly to their objectives. He outlined how each member of the team would contribute and trained them to execute well. From the front-line salespeople to the CEO, all levels of the team knew what to do and how to do it. He got the sales organization to work as a system.

One year into the transition, a leading industry analyst had the opportunity to interview several of the company's clients. The analyst reported back to Randy that the customers he'd spoken with had made a point of discussing how much they appreciated the new way that the company had been selling. The analyst said, "Whatever you're doing, keep doing it. Because your customers notice and value the difference." This unsolicited praise reinforced the fact that it wasn't just *what* the team was selling but *how* they were selling that was registering as a competitive advantage.

The outcomes were dramatic. By the end of the sales leader's first year, the company's total sales went from declining to *increasing by 35 percent*. Sales to new accounts went up 154 percent. Add-on sales increased 133 percent. The total number of sales rose 14.7 percent. Average deal size increased by 18 percent. And for the first time, people who were part of the sales organization were proud to be affiliated with that part of the business. They were engaged, they had an identity, and they had the performance to go along with it.

How does your sales force feel about representing your organization? Are they proud to be affiliated with your brand? Are they clear about your expectations? Are the processes for developing business clear? Have you invested in both the education and tools to help them succeed?

SOLUTIONS HAVE NO INHERENT VALUE

Building a culture that has a focused intent on helping your customers succeed fundamentally changes the way you do business—and requires a different mindset and skillset than has typically been engrained in organizations for the past century. One of the major shifts in mindset that needs to take place is the idea that you should meet the client with the solution in hand. Sales professionals tend to think everyone needs what they have, that their solution is universally applicable. However, solutions only derive value from the problems they solve that people care about, and from producing results that people highly value. Solutions must solve something. If there is nothing the client wants to solve, there is no value to the proposed solution. Understanding this axiom should guide everything you do with clients.

Salespeople are often eager to tell their clients, "The solution to your problem is . . ." Let's take a moment and examine that short phrase. Before reading further, take a couple of minutes and write down the assumptions contained in the phrase:

"The solution to the problem is . . ."

Did you come up with some of these assumptions?

- There is only one problem. There are not multiple problems or several different problems intertwined.
- Likewise, there is only one solution.
- We can measure the extent of the problem.
- The solution would solve the entire problem.
- The cost of the solution is meaningfully less than the cost of the problem.
- Someone is willing and able to allocate sufficient resources to address the problem.

There are a dozen other assumptions you might name. And you could do the same exercise, with similar conclusions, if you substitute the word "opportunity" for the word "problem": "The solution to the opportunity is . . ."

How can you talk intelligently about a solution to a problem without exploring the assumptions involved?

A MUTUAL CONSPIRACY

Nobody likes problems, so there is a mutual conspiracy between buyer and seller to talk about the solution. Sales people love talking about the solution. It is their comfort zone. The solution is what they're selling. They understand it, they know it, it's about them, it's *their* solution, and it's really great. What about the client? They like to believe there is a magic formula—that they can throw some money at the situation and everything will be okay.

It is easier to talk about a solution than to do the critical spadework to uncover the issues the solution is supposed to resolve, to find evidence that proves the client has a problem, to develop metrics for success, to explore systemic implications, and to identify and overcome constraints. Additionally, as long as the solution is the topic of discussion, clients can put all the pressure on the salesperson; they sit back and watch you sing and dance. But since the job to be done now is to bring value to your clients—to help them truly succeed, not just sell your ready-made solution—you must inspire your sales force to go deeper, to look at the issues surrounding the problem.

MOVE OFF THE SOLUTION

Highly effective professionals "move off the solution." While they often begin the conversation with an insightful perspective to interest

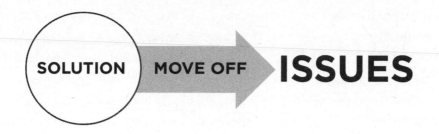

their client, they withhold offering a final solution until they have intelligently explored the problems to be solved and/or the results to be achieved. They organize their questioning to get meaningful answers to critical assumptions. They do so in a way that is comfortable, conversational, and time-efficient. When done well, clients gain insight and understanding of their situation.

But moving off the solution requires discipline and communication skills. One of the hardest behaviors to overcome is the tendency to go for the first solution right off the bat. Sales professionals who can resist the immediate solution are more successful. So move off the solution!

INTENT COUNTS MORE THAN TECHNIQUE

If how you sell matters more than what you sell, then the collective intent of your team members becomes the cornerstone of your sales culture. Technique is still important, but concentrating on the success of others, rather than on your own, is the path to sustainable success. And if you're going to help your clients succeed, you need good information to do it. That means asking questions. Your clients will decide how much information to disclose based largely on their

> If you're going to help your clients succeed, you need good information to do it.

perception of the intent behind your questions. Are you asking questions to help them get what they want in a way they feel good about, or to help *you* get what *you* want in a way *you* feel good about? If they give you information, can they trust that you will use it for their interests and not against them? Many clients make these judgments instinctively, at a subconscious level. Nonetheless, you can influence those judgments.

Trust, as we discussed in Chapter 6, plays a big factor in this. In *The Speed of Trust*, Stephen M. R. Covey makes two key points about the power of intent:

1. **The degree of trust has hard economic consequences**. As trust goes up, speed goes up and costs go down. As trust decreases, everything slows and costs rise. Most of us understand this intuitively; Stephen backs it up with evidence.

2. **Trust can be built on purpose**. Earning trust is a skill that can be learned and improved. It doesn't need to be left to good luck, circumstance, or hope.

In their book *Let's Get Real or Let's Not Play*, Mahan Khalsa and Randy Illig describe trust as follows: Trust = Intent + Expertise. Clients must trust that your intent is compatible with their best interests, and that you have the expertise to design and deliver a solution that meets their needs. For most of us, how we can increase our expertise is far clearer than how we can improve clients' perception of our intent. Yet if clients do not feel comfortable with your intent, they may discount your expertise.

A client will assign an intent to you whether you want them to or not. The intent they assign to you will have a large impact on the quality of your dialogue. If your intent is not crystal clear to you, it may not be clear to the client.

MOVING IN THE WRONG DIRECTION

When people feel they are being manipulated or led to your conclusion rather than their own, they will often move aggressively in the opposite direction. This behavior is called "reactance" or "polarity response." The irony of reactance is that the harder you try to "sell" people, the less likely it is to happen. People feel their choice is being restricted and they become highly motivated to subvert the limitation. It's an emotional response. When trust is compromised, information flow is severely curtailed, and you are far less likely to craft a solution they feel meets their needs.

Conversely, when a client perceives that your intent is to help them succeed, they are more likely to share their beliefs about what that success is. The better you understand what the client wants and needs, the better the choices you can bring to the table. It is in your own best interest to focus on the interests of the client first.

Some part of you understands this dynamic, yet you often feel pressured to meet your personal and organizational revenue goals. Your intent becomes, "Meet the goals! Make the sale!" Perversely, the harder you try, the worse you do. The more important it is to meet your numbers, the more important it is to stop concentrating on *your* numbers and start concentrating on the *clients'* numbers.

> Clients must trust that your intent is compatible with their best interests, and that you have the expertise to design and deliver a solution that meets their needs.

This is something that we and our colleagues know from experience. At times, we have sold to survive ("I've got to get some sales"), we have sold out of ego ("I can get them to do this"), and we have helped clients succeed. We know the difference among these goals in our hearts, minds, and guts. Helping clients succeed not only feels better, it is tremendously more effective.

Helping clients succeed is not an attempt to be nice; it is not philanthropic or selfless; it is a powerful, if paradoxical, means of getting what we want.

A note about technique: Clearly, technique is also important. You could be the most well-intentioned person in the world, a fine human being, yet if you have no communication skills or no critical-thinking tools, you will not be successful. If your technique does not serve your intent, and if that intent does not serve the people you are working with, everything else will be jeopardized.

WORLD-CLASS SALES CULTURES BALANCE ADVOCACY AND INQUIRY

To be in step with what's going on in the selling world today, you can't simply assault a prospect with questions. They're not going to play the game. You can only ask questions after you've earned the right to. Successful business development is a balance between advocacy and inquiry.

> The better you understand what the client wants and needs, the better the choices you can bring to the table. It is in your own best interest to focus on the interests of the client first.

In the past, solution sellers would begin with a potential client by asking a lot of generic questions, and clients were willing to answer the questions. Today, no matter how the process begins—with clients contacting you or you contacting them—you need to be prepared with insightful thinking. Clients will answer your questions, but *only* after they conclude that doing so would be valuable. Clients are looking for salespeople who can help them, who know their business, and who have intelligent thinking to offer. When you can share your good thinking and ask questions that balance advocacy and inquiry, you gain mutual understanding. You have a better understanding of what the client truly values; the client gains better clarity on their own situation and possibilities, and feels understood. The better the job you do of eliciting the client's story, the more able you will be to match your story to theirs.

Most people know how to ask questions and hear what others are saying, yet few are consciously competent at developing a high degree of mutual understanding. They lack either a powerful methodology of questioning, the ability to truly listen with all their senses, or both. Lacking superb inquiry skills (often while thinking that is surely not the case), sales professionals commonly resort to three traditional approaches to interacting with clients:

1. You tell.

When advocacy and inquiry are out of balance, the tilt is almost always toward advocacy. "Telling" is not always bad. Sometimes trusted business advisors help their clients cut through fear, uncertainty, and doubt by strongly advocating what the client must do. You always have telling as a choice. Telling, however, has a low probability of producing a solution that clients feel exactly meets their needs. The downsides of telling include:

You can only ask questions after you've earned the right to.

- What you choose to tell is not interesting or relevant to the client. You waste their time and your own, and reduce the desire for more interactions.

- What you tell them to do might be wrong (it is at least a statistical possibility).

- There may be no buy-in or ownership from the client, which could cause either the sale or the initiative to fail.

- They see you as arrogant, ignorant, or both.

- You potentially leave huge amounts of money on the table by telling clients about one opportunity, when asking them about others could have produced many more.

- You lose the ability to match your story to the client's story, to speak their language, to address their priorities, to foresee and counteract pitfalls early, and to build trust through understanding.

2. You accept.

The client tells you what they want, and you propose to give it to them. Easy, isn't it? Obviously, accepting what the client wants is not always bad, particularly if you agree with them. Yet how often do you propose a solution based on what the client said they wanted, and the client either feels it misses the mark, chooses to do nothing, or picks a solution from a competitor that is different from what they requested? How many times have you won the engagement, given the client what they said they wanted, and still ended up with an unhappy client? The downsides of passively accepting include:

- The client could be wrong—and they will still blame you, sometimes with severe consequences.

- You have not demonstrated any thought leadership.

- You may not understand exactly what you are solving or how to measure success.

- You could leave many opportunities uncovered.

3. You guess.

You may not call it guessing—you may call it diagnosis, assessment, or analysis. Yet if one didn't know better, it would look a lot like guessing. One or two sales professionals talk to one or two client counterparts for an hour or two. Based on that, they start guessing: "What do we think they really need? What do we think the actual problems are? Why haven't they fixed this before now? What should we propose? Do you think we were talking to the right people? Do you think they have any money to pay for this? How much should we charge? Who do you think the competition is?" And so on.

Salespeople, being intelligent, have formalized the guessing process—it's called a proposal. And you can always tell how much salespeople are guessing: the more they guess, the longer the proposal. As the cost of face-to-face business development keeps climbing, the cost of guessing becomes enormous.

> You can always tell how much salespeople are guessing: the more they guess, the longer the proposal.

A Fourth Approach: Mutual Exploration

There is a fourth option: You explore with the client a solution that truly meets their needs—whether they eventually get that solution with you or with someone else. Of course, this is not easy. Clients have come to expect that you will tell, accept, and guess. Even worse, they may try to force you to tell ("You're the expert"), accept ("Just give us what we want"), or guess ("It's all in the RFP").

Mutual exploration has two *imagined* downsides. First, it's believed that it takes more time. However, we assert that mutual exploration does not take more time; it uses time differently and more effectively. If you do not have a solution that meets the client's needs, it is more time effective (and cost effective) to find that out early rather than late. This leads to the second imagined downside: You may find you do not have a solution that truly meets the clients' needs, and thus "lose" a sale. However, consider that you cannot lose something you never had. The probability of selling them something that does not meet their needs is low. Even if they do buy it and only afterward are displeased, you still "lose." Thus, we contend that you can get the upsides of mutual exploration while turning the perceived downsides into advantages.

CREATE A TRUE WIN-WIN SOLUTION

In the new paradigm, sales isn't about selling. It's about helping your clients succeed. This means that your role is to create the conditions for clients to make good decisions—decisions that serve the clients' best interests and help them achieve their highest priorities. It's a paradigm that fully embodies the principle of win-win: The more passionately and skillfully you focus on creating success for your clients, the more successful you will be. This isn't wishful thinking, but a powerful principle that we and our colleagues have seen in action again and again in twenty-five years of research and experience.

As Stephen R. Covey wrote, "Character is the foundation of win-win, and everything else builds on that foundation."[2] In the end, character comes down to one thing: caring as much about others as you do about yourself. If you take the win-win approach, the way you do business becomes your most important distinction in the marketplace. Success is rooted in anticipating and understanding your clients' needs and beliefs, which requires, among other things, empathic listening—a different kind of listening than many of us are used to doing.

> In the end, character comes down to one thing: caring as much about others as you do about yourself.

Covey also wrote, "There are people who protest that empathic listening takes too much time. It may take a little more time initially but it saves so much time downstream. The most efficient thing you can do if you're a doctor and want to prescribe a wise treatment is to make an accurate diagnosis. You can't say, 'I'm in too much of a hurry. I don't have time to make a diagnosis. Just take this treatment.' But when you really listen with a pure desire to understand, you'll be amazed how fast they will open up. They want to open up."[3]

Our friend and colleague Craig Christensen says, "A lot of salespeople hate their jobs because they're being forced to do unnatural things—manipulating, 'hyping,' faking sincerity—it's against their character. We invite them into a place where they can be an advisor to their customers, someone they trust. You don't have to be a jerk, to be tricky and manipulative and pushy. You can invite your customers to take a different journey, and you become a valued business partner."

When the members of a sales organization are operating together in such a culture, they gain synergy and become something exponentially greater than the sum of their parts. Like the everyday students from the University of Washington who together became a team of Olympians, each individual supports and enriches the larger group. The rowers each had very different contributions to make. They had very different sizes, strengths, and capabilities. But by being one in *purpose,* they rowed their way to a gold medal.

The new paradigm is about creating a culture of mutual exploration, and offering the solution that truly meets the client's needs is its goal. It may not happen every time, but it definitely can happen far more often than it does now. There's a change underway, and the leaders who embrace it and create a culture in which win-win selling is a company capability are the leaders who will grant their organization a legacy that is capable of extending today's wins well into the future.

HELPING CLIENTS SUCCEED:
INSTRUCTIONS FOR DOWNLOADING

Here are two sets of exercises to use in building a culture that wins by helping clients succeed. The first lists some key steps that your sales professionals can take with clients—whether external or internal. If you are a sales leader, review these steps with the team until they can understand and commit to them.

STEP	DISCUSSION POINTS
1 CHECK YOUR INTENT	• Write your own personal intent statement in which you define what you are committed to do to ensure that your clients succeed. • You might share your intent with your customer. Clarifying your own personal intent can go a long way toward building trust.
2 MOVE OFF THE SOLUTION	Keep asking questions until you can describe the "win" for your clients better than they can describe it themselves. Listen empathically. Ask about all the ways in which your clients can succeed: • Revenue improvement? • Cost reduction? • Market share? • Return on investment? • Product/service/process improvement? • Risk reduction? • Their own career enhancement? • What else?

STEP	DISCUSSION POINTS
3 — **CREATE A WIN-WIN SOLUTION**	Based on the evidence you've compiled, think creatively about what kind of solution would exactly fit your customer's perception of success.

The second exercise lists the key steps that sales leaders need to take—in order—to institute a superior sales culture. Assess yourself as you review the steps. Do you see your organization doing these things? In this order?

STEP	DISCUSSION POINTS
1 — **CHOOSE YOUR AUDIENCE**	Does your culture focus on salespeople to the exclusion of everyone else in the organization? In reality, the sales force is only one subset of your audience. • Select your audience for your initiative vertically: Include not only the salespeople, but also those to whom they report, and in turn the people to whom they report.

STEP	DISCUSSION POINTS
2 — **DEFINE YOUR TARGET**	• Don't try to take on fifty things at once. If you could hit one or two targets, which ones would really make a difference? • Express your target as "X to Y by When." When you give the effort a clear context—for example, "Increase gross margin from 33 percent to 35 percent by December 31st"—you have a common rallying cry that inspires each individual's effort.
3 — **DESIGN THE TRAINING**	Training is most effective when it simplifies what people are asked to learn to achieve the target. It's also critical to focus on leaders—not just the individual contributors—because leaders will be the advocates and keepers of the sales culture. • What would your training include if you were teaching no more than needed, but leaving out nothing that matters?

4 — **ENGAGED EXECUTION**	When leaders are engaged and can say, "This is my solution," they really take charge and drive the process. • Is your execution expertly designed so that it's easy for continually stretched sales managers to implement? Is it spaced over time?
5 — **MEASURE RESULTS, RINSE, AND REPEAT**	Did you achieve the target you defined earlier? If you're not going to use what you've learned to refine and reengage, then there's no point. • What needs to happen for you to hit the target? • How can you refine and reengage in the process to meet your goal?

CHAPTER 8

PRACTICE 6: CREATE INTENSE LOYALTY

*"You can buy a person's hand, but you can't buy his heart.
His heart is where his enthusiasm, his loyalty is."*

— STEPHEN R. COVEY

I T TOOK RETAIL GIANT COSTCO less than thirty years to become
the second largest retailer in the United States and the seventh
largest in the world—*without advertising*. How? By growing a
worldwide base of intensely loyal customers and employees, many
of whom "wouldn't shop or work anywhere else."

The highest level of engagement is *loyalty*. Loyal workers and
loyal customers are worth their weight in gold. A talented worker
who gives her heart and mind to your enterprise can generate ten- or
a hundred- or a thousand-fold more in revenue and goodwill than
she will ever cost you. A customer who gives you a lifetime of return
business and word-of-mouth support is *the* ultimate competitive
lever you can use to move the world.

The old paradigm was "customer and employee satisfaction." It's
great to have satisfied customers and employees, but it's no longer

enough. The new paradigm is "intense loyalty," and shifting to that paradigm is the job you must do *now*.

"SATISFACTION"—THE OLD PARADIGM

Most customer satisfaction surveys don't lead to meaningful change. They are often poorly designed, too long, and biased. The questions are frequently crafted to get certain answers, which makes the resulting data inaccurate. Many of the questions are centered less on customer issues and more on "How did we do?"

Reliance on pro forma "satisfaction" scores is lazy twentieth-century thinking and a formula for complacency.

Obviously, the quality of leadership is often the reason for loyalty or disloyalty among employees and customers. Reliance on pro forma "satisfaction" scores is lazy twentieth-century thinking and a formula for complacency. The real question for leaders is, "How do you build intense loyalty?"

THE JOB USED TO BE . . .	THE JOB THAT YOU MUST DO NOW . . .
Satisfy customers	Create intense loyalty

"INTENSE LOYALTY": THE NEW PARADIGM

How do you get the kind of intense engagement that was so movingly demonstrated by the workforce at Western Digital? How do you get the unshakable loyalty of sixty million people who gladly fork over a membership fee every year to shop in a warehouse called Costco?

The answer, according to Harvard professor and veteran Bain consultant Fred Reichheld, is "to treat them the way you would want to be treated." This principle, known as the Golden Rule, is laughably simple—and it works. Reichheld cites Colleen Barrett, president emeritus of wildly successful Southwest Airlines: "Practicing the Golden Rule is integral to everything we do." Andy Taylor, executive chairman of Enterprise, the most prosperous rental-car company in the world, says, "The only way to grow is to treat customers so well they come back for more and tell their friends about us."[1]

> "Practicing the Golden Rule is integral to everything we do."
> —COLLEEN BARRETT, PRESIDENT EMERITUS, SOUTHWEST AIRLINES

Here's just one example of Enterprise's appreciation of the Golden Rule: A friend of ours on a business trip got stranded in a small town in the American Midwest. His plane was canceled, and it was long past closing time for the only rental-car office at the tiny airport, but he thought he'd try the door. A smiling young man in a white shirt and tie opened it. He was an Enterprise employee, and quickly signed out the last rental car in town to our friend.

"Why are you even here?" our friend asked. "It's awfully late."

The young man answered, "I heard the flight out of town got canceled, so I figured somebody would probably need me." Then he pulled a cake out of his small refrigerator. "My wife made this cake today and brought it over for anybody who might want some. Would you like a piece?" Our friend had missed his dinner and actually was kind of hungry. He thankfully took the piece on a plate with a fork and a napkin, and it was delicious.

Then the young man said, "Here, take the whole cake. You've got a long drive to Des Moines."

Our friend, who had never done business with Enterprise before, is now a lifetime customer. "They take the cake!" he says. Enterprise systematically instills the Golden Rule into every one of its nearly 70,000 employees, and as a result is named the most customer-friendly car rental company year after year.

> **Study after study demonstrates that customer loyalty is the prime driver of profitable growth.**

Every company has pockets of great customer service, but few make a system of it—which is ironic, since study after study demonstrates that customer loyalty is the prime driver of profitable growth. It's well established that as little as 5 percent growth in customer loyalty can drive as much as 85 percent growth in profits.[2]

By contrast, chronic inconsistencies in customer service are the enemy of loyalty. Some companies pay a fearsome price when their poor practices show up on YouTube—a delivery person carelessly tossing a customer's purchases into his truck, workers stealing photos off a customer's laptop, a fast-food employee licking the food. You can't afford an inconsistent record when it comes to promoting loyalty. Of course, the opposite is also true—stories of extraordinary customer service can spread like wildfire.

AN INTENSE-LOYALTY "APP"

Companies need a *system*—an "application"—for building loyalty all along the journey of the client or employee. For a long time, leaders have focused on improving "moments of truth," touch points where customers might come in contact with the firm. This is helpful, but it produces excellence only in spots. Researchers say, "Organizations able to skillfully manage the entire customer experience reap enormous rewards: enhanced customer satisfaction, reduced churn, increased revenue, and greater employee satisfaction too."[3]

A loyalty "app" starts with both customer and employee loyalty measures. Many organizations are now using Reichheld's well-regarded "Net Promoter Score" as their key measure of both. It's the ratio between people who would recommend your company as a great place to work or do business and those who definitely would not. If your score is 100, everyone recommends you; if it's –100, nobody does. A score of 50 or more is unusually high because you have many more promoters than detractors.

The Net Promoter Score provides a credible baseline measurement of loyalty, but you need other information to tell you what to *do* about your score. That information comes from careful analysis of customer input—in other words, empathic listening. What is the customer or employee telling you specifically about yourself? What things do they specify when praising you or complaining about you? From this analytical work you can isolate the lead measures to address. Leaders who combine a true measure of loyalty like the Net Promoter Score with a rich system of input are most likely to know what to do to improve that score. Once you know the score, you can make leaps in loyalty a wildly important goal—and you should.

Powerful Lead Measures: Fascinated People

As we discussed in Chapter 4, lead measures track actions you take to achieve a goal, and lag measures quantify the results. Some organizations have powerful lead measures for driving loyalty among all stakeholders. One unique company is Grupo Entero of Guatemala City, a diverse and thriving enterprise started by Juan Mauricio Bonifasi, known as "Juanma." A careful student of the 7 Habits for some years, Juanma conceived of a company that would be based on their principles, a company where proactive, visionary people could flourish. Juanma doesn't distinguish between clients and employees—they are all *colaboradores*, or contributors.

"Our primary goal," he says, "is to fascinate our contributors, to create a culture where people are fulfilled by using their talents in passions in their work."

Grupo Entero is essentially a holding company, a nursery for entrepreneurial businesses staffed with *fascinados*—fascinated people. One branch of the company is Guateprenda, a microcredit bank that lends money to low-income borrowers who want to start their own businesses. No traditional bank would lend to such people. But just a small loan can make a huge difference to a farmer who needs a truck for his market garden or a single mother who could make a lot more money selling snow cones if she had more equipment and a storefront. Guateprenda's people become emotional when they talk about the tremendous difference they are making throughout Central America. Another Grupo Entero undertaking is Sonrié, a chain of dental clinics "dedicated to freeing people from pain and helping them maximize their potential." The staffers at Sonrié work miracles for suffering children and disfigured adults who gain new confidence in the workplace.

> "Our primary goal is to fascinate our contributors, to create a culture where people are fulfilled by using their talents in passions in their work."
> —JUAN MAURICIO BONIFASI, FOUNDER, GRUPO ENTERO

We're enthralled by Juanma's notion that each individual associated with his Grupo Entero, whether client or employee, is considered a *colaborador*, a *fascinado* who is finding an outlet for his or her passion and potential. It's a remarkable business model—a company that exists not just to make money!—although Grupo Entero thrives financially as people clamor to be part of an enterprise dedicated to unleashing the potential of every contributor. He and his fellow leaders heavily invest their time and money to understand and develop that potential so it can be leveraged. Every contributor is thoroughly trained in the 7 Habits, the mental operating system of the company, and then a development plan is tailored carefully for him or her, a plan that will leverage the individual's fascination in life. Grupo Entero's whole purpose is to see those dreams realized.

A Loss of Productivity: Passionless People

Contrast Grupo Entero with the development practices of most organizations. "It's hard to think of an important aspect of management more neglected than development planning: helping your employees shape the future direction of their careers," says business executive and writer Victor Lipman. "Yet this valuable activity is ignored . . . or handled as a bureaucratic exercise . . . or an afterthought. Companies pay a high price: the loss of top young talent." How many leaders give it even a thought?[4]

"People care if you take a genuine interest in their future," says Lipman. "Taking an honest interest in someone builds loyalty. Loyal employees are more engaged. Engaged employees are more productive."[5]

> "People care if you take a genuine interest in their future . . . Taking an honest interest in someone builds loyalty.
> —VICTOR LIPMAN

EMPLOYEE LOYALTY LEADS TO CUSTOMER LOYALTY

It's also fascinating to note how employee loyalty affects customer loyalty, which in turn affects the bottom line. "One lesson that emerges from the experience of low-end retailers is that putting workers in crummy, low-wage jobs tends to yield crummy service as well," wrote journalist Harold Myerson.[6] This was demonstrated when a large US home-improvement retailer cut costs by eliminating its experienced floor staff as well as its educational programs, resulting in the inexperienced staff that was left not being trained properly to service customers. Following suit, the company's reputation for excellent customer service collapsed and sales slowed to a crawl.[7]

By contrast, companies that work to gain the intense loyalty of their employees tend also to gain the intense loyalty of their customers. Grupo Entero embodies this principle with its philosophy of cultivating loyal contributors. As we mentioned, Costco's miraculous rise likewise is due to the loyalty of its contributors. The firm pays its people 42 percent more than average for the industry and provides an enviable package of benefits, including career education and a ladder to the top. Employee turnover is 6 percent, contrasted with around 40 percent for the retail sector as a whole. Upbeat Costco employees look like they enjoy their work, and in the view of brand expert David Aaker, Costco's company policy clearly results in customer loyalty.[8]

That loyalty is intense and growing. As of this writing, Costco's Net Promoter Score is an astounding 71, the highest in the retail industry.[9] Millions of shoppers pack Costco stores across eight nations, according to ABC's *20/20,* "and for some of them the experience borders on the spiritual. Shopper Jose Davila put it this way: 'This is the best place in the world. It's like going to church. You can't get anything better than this. This is a religious experience.'"[10]

> When leaders focus on workers as people, on customers as people—while keeping an eye on profitability—they cannot help but succeed.

To put things a little more modestly, Costco's leaders are living by the simple principle of treating people the way they themselves would like to be treated. A friend of ours, a local attorney, goes with his wife to Costco every Saturday morning "because that is where I see all my friends." For him, shopping is important, but the overall experience is the real story. It keeps bringing him back. In the end, when leaders focus on workers as people, on customers as people—while keeping an eye on profitability—they cannot help but succeed.

MOVING THE MIDDLE

As far as we know, no organization has ever earned a Net Promoter Score of 100. Getting into the seventies puts you among an elite few companies, like Costco, because the average score is between 10 and 15.[11] If you're a leader, one of your wildly important goals is to raise your company's score, whatever it is, because of the critical value of stakeholder loyalty. A realistic strategy for doing that, whether you're leading a small team or a whole company, is to "move the middle."

Any business has promoters and detractors. Some promoters (like your mother) will love you no matter what you do. Some detractors (hopefully not your mother) will hate you no matter what you do. You're not likely to affect the feelings of people at either end of the spectrum, but in the middle is the vast majority who could be influenced. If you can move that group even a few points toward the promoter side of the spectrum, you reap huge dividends because the group is so large.

A revolutionary study by the Sales Executive Council has shown that a mere 5 percent performance gain from the middle 60 percent of a sales force yielded, on average, more than 70 percent more revenue than a 5 percent shift in the top 20 percent of employees.[12] In simple terms, a small movement in the middle has an effect on the top line that is way out of proportion.

Anything you can do to move the middle toward intense loyalty will reap big benefits. Often passive customers can become very loyal customers if you listen with empathy to their issues. For example, Shawn says, "I'm very happy with my tablet. I love it. I'm a 'middling' user—I enjoy getting Wi-Fi access to my favorite social media and

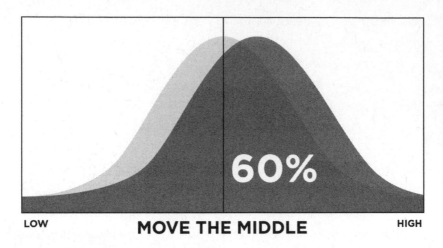

LOW   **MOVE THE MIDDLE**   HIGH

Move the Middle

news sites and an occasional movie, but I'm neither a techie early adopter nor a cranky old Luddite. I'm just loyal to my tablet.

"But if I were asked, I do have a few issues with it. I'd like to have a protective case that isn't so heavy. I get knocked off my applications too often. I know I have to sync it, but I wish I didn't. The app store is hard for me to navigate. And sometimes the connection problems make me want to throw it out the window.

> **Often passive customers can become very loyal customers if you listen with empathy to their issues.**

"I recognize my issues are petty and unreasonable, but tablet-computer designers who are also empathic listeners might be able to help. And if they did, my loyalty to their product would zoom up into the intensity zone."

THE INTENSITY ZONE

Because the rewards of intense loyalty are so great, you should be gripped by the goal of achieving the "intensity zone," where people wouldn't want to work or do business with anyone but you. Who can calculate the value of workers who will wade through the mud for each other and their company? Or the value of customers who feel almost religiously tied to you? Moving the most people possible toward the intensity zone should be a wildly important goal for every leader, and is the job you must do now.

CREATING INTENSE LOYALTY: INSTRUCTIONS FOR DOWNLOADING

STEP	DISCUSSION POINTS
1 MEASURE YOUR CUSTOMER AND EMPLOYEE LOYALTY	One way to do this is to calculate the Net Promoter Score. • Ask this question: "On a scale from 0 to 10 (with 10 being high), how likely is it that you would recommend us to a friend or colleague? Please give your reasons for your answer." • Categorize the scores as follows: **Score Category** 9–10 Promoters: Loyal, enthusiastic, will give you return business and refer others. 7–8 Passives: Satisfied but not enthusiastic, vulnerable to competitors. 0–6 Detractors: Unhappy, will give you negative word of mouth. • To calculate the Net Promoter Score, subtract the percentage who are detractors from the percentage who are promoters.

STEP	DISCUSSION POINTS
2 — SET A GOAL TO IMPROVE YOUR LOYALTY MEASURE	• Set a wildly important goal to improve the Net Promoter Score. Choose a number that you think is attainable and give yourself a deadline to achieve it.
3 — ACT ON YOUR LEAD MEASURES	• Analyze carefully the reasons the respondents gave for their choices. Look for recurring themes. • Drill deeper into those recurring themes. Get on the phone and social media and go talk to customers and employees face to face. Get to the bottom of the issues people are raising about you. • As a team, select lead measures based on the themes you've discovered. • Act on the lead measures and carefully track your progress.

Conclusion: The Job for You to Do Now Starts Today

"A blank page is no empty space. It is brimming with potential. It is a masterpiece in waiting—yours."

—A. A. Patawaran

IN THIS BOOK WE'VE SEEN how your people—the ultimate source of competitive advantage—can become highly effective leaders at every level of the organization. We've learned how leaders can create engagement by connecting to the "voice of the organization," how critical it is to execute with excellence, how doing so will result in our talent contributing infinitely more than we could imagine, the economic value of becoming the most trusted company in our industry, how sales can create and increase revenue by focusing on clients' success, and how and why increasing intense loyalty both inside the organization and in the market impacts results and growth. A culture that puts these practices in place will create a highly effective organization, and that's the kind of organization we all want to work in and that you need to create now.

In the past, it was probably enough to be a good manager, figuring out how to do more with less, adding value, and making sure your customers and employees were satisfied. But no more. It's time to move beyond the mindset that every team member's role, and yours, should be prescribed and you all should subscribe to it. That way of thinking doesn't ask enough of our hearts or brains. It's more of a clock-in/clock-out mentality—insert your job description into your head in the morning and eject it in the evening. Under that system, the job to be done is programmed for you.

THE NEW JOB TO BE DONE NOW

That system had its place, but now our lives are far more exacting—and also more fascinating. Everyone can be a leader. In fact, individual leadership is an imperative! The way is open for people to make an infinitely more significant contribution than they ever imagined they could. The mission is to achieve your own great purpose by helping others achieve theirs. The maxim now is *meaning*.

> The mission is to achieve your own great purpose by helping others achieve theirs. The maxim now is *meaning*.

The leader's job has changed fundamentally. The mental operating system is no longer "control" but "unleash." It's founded in purpose and principles instead of compliance and calculation. Dee Hock, the innovative leader who created the Visa card, describes this mindset: "To the degree that you hold purpose and principles in common among you, you can dispense with command and control. People will know how to behave in accordance with them, and they'll do it in thousands of unimaginable, creative ways. The organization will become a vital, living set of beliefs."[1]

Too much of the old mindset persists. Until we choose to be empathic, we'll continue to lead from an inner core of indifference, but people know instinctively when they're being stage-managed. "Leaders are often tossed and turned," said Stephen R. Covey. "Should they be more democratic or more autocratic? Firmer or more permissive? Tell more or ask more? What are the best techniques for getting things done through and with people? These questions are important and must be considered, but they are secondary questions. The primary question is: How much do you really care?"

Do you care enough to do what is required?

To make the choice to be a *leader*, not just a job description?

To help others become leaders? To install an operating system that enables leaders at all levels?

To unleash people to contribute infinitely more than you imagined they could?

To execute your most important goals with excellence and precision?

To become the most trusted of leaders?

To help your customers succeed in their own great purposes?

To create intense loyalty among the people you serve?

These are the tough but exhilarating choices leaders have to make now. In this book, we have walked through the principles, the paradigms, and the practices of this new kind of leadership. If you make good use of them, you'll be equal to the challenge of becoming a true leader.

DON'T GIVE UP

But what if you don't *feel* equal to the challenge? What if you're afraid to make that choice because of the weight of organizational politics? You may be thinking, "What will they say if I suddenly become proactive and visionary and empathic? How will they react if I start saying 'no' to things that don't matter much so I can say 'yes' to things that do? What will happen if I question a strategy or policy that won't help the client succeed? Will they even *let* me be a leader?"

Whoever "they" are, don't worry about them.

More than a century ago, researchers at Clark University did an experiment with a walleye pike, a very aggressive fish. The researchers placed the pike in a large tank filled with water and added several minnows, the pike's natural food, then watched as the minnows were immediately devoured. The researchers then placed a transparent glass divider in the tank with new minnows on one side and the pike on the other. Again the larger fish went after the minnows, this time hitting its head against the glass with each attempt. Eventually, the pike stopped trying to eat the minnows, having learned that the effort would only bring a sore head.

After three months, the researchers removed the glass barrier. Now there was nothing separating the predator from its prey. Yet even with the minnows now swimming all around the tank, the pike made no attempt to eat them. The pike would starve to death before trying to eat its favorite meal.[2] Such is the power of discouragement (or a sore head!). We may have tried and failed in the past, and because we learned that trying can occasionally bring failure and pain, we assume it will always be so.

Don't believe it.

If you choose to focus your energy on the things you *can* do something about, your influence grows—often dramatically.

When you focus your energy on things you can't control, your influence shrinks. You may still be worried about politics, your position with this or that person, who's getting promoted or demoted, or who's up, down, or sideways. But this is debilitating thinking that will only diminish your capacity to contribute.

By contrast, if you choose to focus your energy on the things you *can* do something about, your influence grows—often dramatically. You can't control what others do; you can only hope to *influence* them. You contribute what you can instead of exhausting your energy in futile political games because your allegiance is to the principles, not to the players.

You will make mistakes. All leaders do. You may feel awkward at first, but if you persist, you will eventually feel the excitement of real growth in yourself, your team, and the bottom line.

This book began with two stories: the heroic account of a highly engaged team in Thailand, and the story of a guy named Tom who had stopped contributing. His body was going to work but his mind and heart were elsewhere. He had allowed an autocratic system void of vision or purpose to siphon away his passion and energy.

You don't have to be Tom. You can choose to be a proactive leader and bring vision and purpose to your work. You can be the leader of a team every bit as engaged as the people who resurrected Western Digital.

As noted author and Harvard professor Rosabeth Moss Kanter says, "A vision is not just a picture of what could be; it is an appeal to our better selves, a call to become something more."[3] So what is your picture of what could be? What is your "something more"?

Let's get started.

To view video case studies of the examples noted in this book as well as several other client case studies, go to www.franklincovey.com/uca.

ENDNOTES

CHAPTER 1

[1] "Anson Dorrance," *GoHeels.com,* accessed August 2, 2014, http://www.goheels.com/ViewArticle.dbml?ATCLID=205497928.

[2] Peter M. Senge, *The Fifth Discipline: The Art & Practice of the Learning Organization* (New York: Currency, 1990), 132

[3] Tom Felix Joehnk, "Wading in Thailand's Murky Waters," *Latitude* (blog), *The New York Times,* November 14, 2011, http://latitude.blogs.nytimes.com/2011/11/14/wading-in-thailands-murky-waters/?_r=0.

[4] Gallup, Inc., *State of the American Workplace: Employee Engagement Insights for U.S. Business Leaders,* 2013, http://www.gallup.com/strategicconsulting/163007/state-american-workplace.aspx.

[5] David F. Larcker et al., *2013 CEO Performance Evaluation Survey* (Stanford, CA: Stanford Graduate School of Business, Center for Leadership Development and Research, 2013), http://www.gsb.stanford.edu/cldr/research/surveys/performance.html; Susan Adams, "CEOs Are Terrible at Management, Study Finds," *Forbes,* May 23, 2013, http://www.forbes.com/sites/susanadams/2013/05/23/ceos-are-terrible-at-management-study-finds.

[6] Michael Porter, *Competitive Advantage: Creating and Sustaining Superior Performance* (New York: Free Press, 1998), xix, italics added.

[7] Ibid, xviii, italics added.

[8] Clayton M. Christensen, James Allworth, and Karen Dillon, *How Will You Measure Your Life?* (New York: HarperBusiness, 2012), 160.

[9] Stacy Conradt, "11 of the Best Customer Service Stories Ever," *Mental Floss,* March 12, 2012, http://mentalfloss.com/article/30198/11-best-customer-service-stories-ever.

[10] Christensen et al., *How Will You Measure Your Life?,* 166.

CHAPTER 2

[1] Stephen R. Covey, *The 7 Habits of Highly Effective People* (New York: Simon & Schuster, 2013), 6.

[2] "How to Set Goals for Employees," *The Wall Street Journal*, n.d., http://guides.wsj.com/management/strategy/how-to-set-goals/.

[3] Seth Godin, "Choosing to Be Formidable," *Seth's Blog,* Aug. 9, 2013. http://sethgodin.typepad.com/seths_blog/2013/08/choosing-to-be -formidable.html.

[4] Bernice Anderson Poole, *Mary McLeod Bethune: Educator (Black American Series)* (Los Angeles: Melrose Square Publishing, 1994), 145.

[5] Deborah Gillan Straub, "Mary McLeod Bethune," in *Contemporary Heroes and Heroines Book II,* eds. Deborah Gillan Straub et al. (Detroit, MI: Gale Research, 1992), 151–52.

[6] Lou Gerstner, *Who Says Elephants Can't Dance? Leading a Great Enterprise through Dramatic Change* (New York: HarperBusiness, 2003), 71.

[7] Justin Fox, "How Shareholders Are Ruining American Business," *Atlantic Monthly*, June 19, 2013, http://www.theatlantic.com /magazine/archive/2013/07/stop-spoiling-the-shareholders/309381/.

[8] Poole, *Mary McLeod Bethune,* 130, 152–53.

[9] Kaihan Krippendorff, "The Jack Welch Leadership Crash Course," *Fast Company*, October 25, 2012, http://www.fastcompany .com/3002406/jack-welch-leadership-crash-course.

[10] "How to Set Goals for Employees," *The Wall Street Journal,* n.d., http://guides.wsj.com/management/strategy/how-to-set-goals/.

[11] David Fishwick, "Why I Opened a 'Bank,'" *Huffington Post UK,* November 7, 2012, http://www.huffingtonpost.co.uk/david-fishwick /bank-of-dave-why-i-opened   it_b_1664967.html?just_reloaded=1; David Harrison, "The Bank of Dave," *MailOnline*, June 23, 2012, http://www.dailymail.co.uk/femail/article-2163604/Dave-Fishwick -How-self-millionaire-helped-firms-unable-loans-home-town.html.

[12] "Power Women: #49 Angela Ahrendts," *Forbes,* May 28, 2013, http://www.forbes.com/profile/angela-ahrendts.

[13] Kathy Gersch and John Kotter, "Burberry's Secrets to Successful Brand Reinvention," *Forbes*, February 26, 2013, http://

www.forbes.com/sites/johnkotter/2013/02/26/burberrys-secrets -to-successful-brand-reinvention.

[14] Nandani Lynton, "Managing the Chinese Way," *McKinsey Quarterly*, July 2013, http://www.mckinsey.com/insights/asia-pacific /managing_the_chinese_way.

[15] Ibid.

[16] Heidi Grant Halvorson and E. Tory Higgins, *Focus: Use Different Ways of Seeing the World for Success and Influence* (New York: Hudson Street Press, 2013).

[17] Hamid Bouchikhi and John R. Kimberly, "Making Mergers Work" (summary), *MIT Sloan Management Review*, September 18, 2012, http://sloanreview.mit.edu/article/making-mergers-work.

[18] Bastian Schaefer, "A 3D-Printed Jumbo Jet?", TEDGlobal 2013 video, 5:58, June 2013, http://www.ted.com/talks/bastian_schaefer_a_3d _printed_jumbo_jet.html.

[19] Bob Hancké, *Large Firms and Institutional Change,* (Oxford, UK: Oxford University Press, 2002), 141–78.

[20] J. V. Kovach, E. A. Cudney, and C. C. Elrod, "The Use of Continuous Improvement Techniques: A Survey-Based Study of Current Practices," *International Journal of Engineering, Science and Technology* 3, no. 7 (2011), 89–100.

[21] Harold Leavitt, *Top Down: Why Hierarchies Are Here to Stay and How to Manage Them More Effectively* (Boston: Harvard Business Review Press, 2004), 67.

[22] Jeremy Pearce, "Harold J. Leavitt, 85, Management Expert, Dies," *The New York Times,* December 26, 2007, http://www.nytimes .com/2007/12/26/business/26leavitt.html?_r=0.

[23] "Leaders Everywhere: A Conversation with Gary Hamel," McKinsey & Company Insights & Publications, video, 9:51, May 2013, http:// www.mckinsey.com/insights/organization/leaders_everywhere_a _conversation_with_gary_hamel.

[24] Larcker et al., *CEO Performance Evaluation Survey 2013.*

[25] "Captain Denny Flanagan—Friendlier Skies," *Carolina Travel Girl* (blog), October 16, 2013, http://first2board.com/carolinatravelgirl/2013 /10/16/captain-denny-flanagan-friendlier-skies.

[26] Covey, *The 7 Habits,* 4.

[27] McKinsey & Company, "Leaders Everywhere."

CHAPTER 3

[1] Sarah Sturtevant, "Lessons From a Dabbawala," *Marketing Masala* (blog), June 10, 2009, http://sarahsturtevant.com/wordpress/branding /lessons-from-a-dabbawala/.

[2] *State of the American Workplace: Employee Engagement Insights for U.S. Business Leaders,* The Gallup Organization, 2013, http://www.gallup .com/strategicconsulting/163007/state-american-workplace.aspx.

[3] Seth Godin, "Your Manifesto, Your Culture," Seth's Blog, April 24, 2013, http://sethgodin.typepad.com/seths_blog/2013/04/your-manifesto -your-culture.html.

[4] Stephen R. Covey, *The 8th Habit: From Effectiveness to Greatness* (New York: Simon & Schuster, 2004), 5.

[5] Ibid., 5.

[6] Mark C. Crowley, "How SAS Became the World's Best Place to Work," *FastCompany,* January 22, 2013, http://www.fastcompany .com/3004953/how-sas-became-worlds-best-place-work.

[7] "Doing Well by Being Rather Nice," *The Economist,* November 29, 2007, http://www.economist.com/node/10208507.

[8] Rebecca Leung, "Working the Good Life," *60 Minutes,* April 18, 2003, http://www.cbsnews.com/news/working-the-good-life.

[9] Crowley, "SAS."

[10] SAS Institute, 2012 Corporate Responsibility Report, http://www .sas.com/company/csr_reports/archive/csr-report-current.pdf.

[11] Paul S. Goodman, "The Cult of the Dabbawala," *The Economist,* July 10, 2008, www.economist.com/node/11707779.

[12] Karl Moore, "The Best Way to Innovation? An Important Lesson from India," *Forbes,* May 24, 2011, http://www.forbes.com/sites/karl moore/2011/05/24/the-best-way-to-innovation-an-important-lesson -from-india/; Sue Gillman, "4 Reasons the Dabbawala Supply Chain Succeeds While Corporate Giants Struggle," *iSixSigma* (blog), July 8, 2011, http://www.isixsigma.com/community/blogs/4-reasons-dabbawala -supply-chain-succeeds-while-corporate-giants-struggle.

[13] Saritha Rai, "In India, Grandma Cooks, They Deliver," *The New York Times*, May 29, 2007, http://www.nytimes.com/2007/05/29/business/worldbusiness/29lunch.html?pagewanted=1&_r=1.

[14] Goodman, "The Cult of the Dabbawala."

CHAPTER 4

[1] "Three Reasons Why Good Strategies Fail: Execution, Execution, Execution," *Knowledge@Wharton* (blog), August 10, 2005, http://knowledge.wharton.upenn.edu/article.cfm?articleid=1252.

[2] See Chris McChesney, Sean Covey, and Jim Huling, *The 4 Disciplines of Execution: Achieving Your Wildly Important Goals* (New York: Free Press, 2012).

[3] Scott Briscoe, "Measures of Greatness: An Interview with Jim Collins," *Associations Now*, November 2006, http://www.asaecenter.org/Resources/ANowDetail.cfm?ItemNumber=20825.

[4] "Three Reasons."

[5] "Making the Emotional Case for Change: An Interview with Chip Heath," *McKinsey Quarterly*, March 2010, http://www.mckinsey.com/insights/organization/making_the_emotional_case_for_change_an_interview_with_chip_heath.

[6] Chris McChesney and Jim Huling, "Four Reasons Why Your 2013 Strategy Will Fail (and What to Do about It)," *Forbes*, January 25, 2013, http://www.forbes.com/sites/forbesleadershipforum/2013/01/25/four-reasons-why-your-2013-strategy-will-fail/.

[7] "Three Reasons."

[8] W. Gibb Dyer Jr., Jeffrey H. Dyer, and William G. Dyer, *Team Building: Proven Strategies for Improving Performance*, 5th ed. (Hoboken, NJ: John Wiley & Sons, 2013), 120–21.

[9] "Leaders Everywhere."

[10] Kristen Zambo and Andre Salles, "Aurora Leaders Target Crime, Development, Neighborhoods for 2007," *The Beacon-News–Aurora (IL)*, February 15, 2007, http://www.highbeam.com/doc/1N1-118383ABA5340088.html.

[11] Dean W. Collinwood and Sangita Skilling, "Changing Colors at Leighs Paints," FranklinCovey Center for Advanced Research,

February 2009, http://www.franklincoveyresearch.org/catalog/CFR 090196_LeiPai_CasStu__v1.0.4__lr.pdf.

CHAPTER 5

[1] Ron Breazeale, "Your Job," *In the Face of Adversity* (blog), *Psychology Today,* April 1, 2013, http://www.psychologytoday.com/blog /in-the-face-adversity/201304/your-job.

[2] Donna Jackson Nakazawa, "The American Stress-Illness Crisis," *The Last Best Cure* (blog), *Psychology Today*, May 13, 2013, http://www.psychologytoday.com/blog/the-last-best-cure/201305 /the-american-stress-illness-crisis.

[3] Larissa Faw, "Why Some Women Are Burning Out at Work at 30," *Forbes*, November 22, 2011, http://www.nbcnews.com/id/45357267 /ns/business-forbes_com/t/why-some-women-are-burning-out -work/?fb_ref=.TsvEvx98ch4.like&fb_source=home_multiline# .Ugbz8pKsim7.

[4] "Are You Suffering from Job Burnout"? *CareerBuilder UK*, August 26, 2011, http://www.careerbuilder.co.uk/Article/CB-361 -Workplace-Issues-Are-you-suffering-from-job-burnout.

[5] Panjak Singh, "Health Consequences and Buffers of Burnout Among Indian Software Developers," *Psychological Studies*, Nov. 2, 2012, http:// link.springer.com/article/10.1007%2Fs12646-012-0171-9#page-2.

[6] Yasmin Taj, "India Inc. in Need of an Anti-Stress Pill," *The Economic Times,* Apr. 2, 2013, http://epaper.timesofindia.com/Repository /getFiles.asp?Style=OliveXLib:LowLevelEntityToPrint_ETNEW &Type=text/html&Locale=english-skin-custom&Path=ETD /2013/04/02&ID=Ar01400.

[7] Jane Weaver, "Job Stress, Burnout on the Rise," *NBC News,* September 1, 2003, http://www.nbcnews.com/id/3072410/ns/business-us _business/t/job-stress-burnout-rise/#.Ugb7lpKsim4.

[8] Peter Bisson, Elizabeth Stephenson, and S. Patric Viguerie, "The Productivity Imperative," McKinsey & Company, June 2010, http:// www.mckinsey.com/insights/growth/the_productivity_imperative.

[9] Towers Perrin, *"Turbocharging" Employee Engagement: The Power of Recognition from Managers, Part 2—The Circle of Recognition,* 2010,http://www.towerswatson.com/en-US/Insights/IC-Types/Survey

-Research-Results/2009/12/Turbocharging-Employee-Engagement -The-Power-of-Recognition-From-Managers-Part-2.

[10] Adam Grant, "What Millennials Really Want Out of Work," *Huffington Post Blog,* August 2, 2013, http://www.huffingtonpost.com/adam -grant/millennial-generation-jobs_b_3696622.html. Italics added.

[11] Tamarra Kemsley, "Human Body Distinguishes between 'Hedonic' and 'Eudaimonic' Happiness on Molecular Level," *Nature World News,* July 30, 2013, http://www.natureworldnews.com/articles/3242 /20130730/human-body-distinguishes-between-hedonic-eudaimonic -happiness-molecular-level.htm.

[12] Barbara Frederickson et al., "A Functional Genomic Perspective on Human Well-being," *Proceedings of the National Academy of Sciences* 11, no. 33 (2013): 13684–13689, http://www.pnas.org/content /110/33/13684.full.

[13] Daniel H. Pink, *Drive: The Surprising Truth About What Motivates Us* (New York: Penguin, 2011), 223.

[14] Peter F. Drucker, *Management,* rev. ed. (New York: HarperBusiness, 2008), 191.

[15] The six-year study was between 2005 and 2011. It was based on 351,613 respondents from Africa, the Asia-Pacific region, Europe, Latin America, the Middle East, and North America.

[16] W. H. Murray, *The Scottish Himalayan Expedition* (London: J. M. Dent, 1951).

[17] "The New Organisation," *The Economist,* January 19, 2006, 3, http://www.economist.com/node/5380483.

[18] Gavin Newsom and Lisa Dickey, *Citizenville* (New York: Penguin Press, 2013), 11.

[19] Dave Meslin, "The Antidote to Apathy," TEDxToronto 2010 video, 7:05, October 2010, http://www.ted.com/talks/dave_meslin _the_antidote_to_apathy.

CHAPTER 6

[1] Jeanette Mulvey, "American Workers Don't Trust Their Bosses," *BusinessNewsDaily,* July 12, 2011, http://www.businessnewsdaily .com/1195-employees-dont-trust-bosses.html.

[2] Geoffrey James, "Warning: Customers Don't Trust Leaders," *Inc.*, April 19, 2013, http://www.inc.com/geoffrey-james/warning-customers -dont-trust-leaders.html.

[3] The University of Chicago Booth School of Business, "Chicago Booth/Kellogg School Financial Trust Index Finds Anger over Economy Remains Even as Trust and Optimism Remain," *Chicago Booth/ Kellogg School Financial Trust Index,* May 31, 2013, http://www.chicago booth.edu/about/newsroom/press-releases/2013/2013-05-31.

[4] Leigh Branham, *The 7 Hidden Reasons Employees Leave* (New York: AMACOM, 2012), 188.

[5] Colin Mayer, *Firm Commitment: Why the Corporation Is Failing Us and How to Restore Trust in It* (Oxford, UK: Oxford University Press, 2013).

[6] Watson Wyatt, "Human Capital Index," *WorkUSA* (Arlington, VA: Watson Wyatt, 2002).

[7] Cited in Ronald J. Burke, Edward C. Tomlinson, and Cary L. Cooper, *Crime and Corruption in Organizations: Why It Occurs and What to Do About It* (Surrey, UK: Gower Publishing, 2012), 176.

[8] Newsom, *Citizenville,* 12.

[9] Cheryl Hall, "Frito-Lay Puts Trust in Trust," *Dallas Morning News,* March 9, 2011, http://www.dallasnews.com/business/columnists /cheryl-hall/20110308-frito-lay-puts-trust-in-trust.ece.

[10] "Al Carey, CEO of Frito-Lay, on *The Speed of Trust*," YouTube video, 1:50, posted by "Franklincovey Speedoftrust," July 5, 2011, http:// www.youtube.com/watch?v=JZqK3MKxbpo.

[11] See Stephen M. R. Covey, *The Speed of Trust: The One Thing That Changes Everything* (New York: Free Press, 2006).

CHAPTER 7

[1] Daniel James Brown, *The Boys in the Boat: Nine Americans and Their Epic Quest for Gold at the 1936 Berlin Olympics* (New York: Viking, 2013), 2.

[2] Covey, *The 7 Habits*, 217.

[3] Ibid., 252.

CHAPTER 8

[1] Fred Reichheld, *The Ultimate Question: Driving Good Profits and True Growth* (Boston: Harvard Business School Press, 2006), 14.

[2] James L. Heskett et al., "Putting the Service-Profit Chain to Work," *Harvard Business Review*, March 1994, http://hbr.org/1994/03 /putting-the-service-profit-chain-to-work/ar/1.

[3] Alex Rawson, Ewan Duncan, and Conor Jones, "The Truth about Customer Experience," *Harvard Business Review*, September 2013, http://hbr.org/2013/09/the-truth-about-customer-experience/ar/1.

[4] Victor Lipman, "Why Employee Development Is Important but Neglected," *Mind of the Manager* (blog), *Psychology Today*, March 13, 2013, http://www.psychologytoday.com/blog/mind-the-manager/201303 /why-employee-development-is-important-neglected.

[5] Ibid.

[6] Harold Meyerson, "Taking the 'Service' Out of the Service Sector," *Washington Post*, April 16, 2013, http://articles.washingtonpost.com /2013-04-16/opinions/38584154_1_wal-mart-u-s-workforce-ron -johnson.

[7] Zeynep Ton, "Why 'Good Jobs' Are Good for Retailers," *Harvard Business Review*, January–February 2012, http://hbr.org/2012/01 /why-good-jobs-are-good-for-retailers.

[8] Wayne F. Cascio, "The High Cost of Low Wages," *Harvard Business Review*, December 2006, http://hbr.org/2006/12/the-high-cost-of -low-wages/ar/1; David Aaker, "Can Employee Policy Lead to Customer Loyalty? Costco and HP Prove It Can," *Prophet*, July 10, 2013, www.prophet.com/blog/aakeronbrands/148-can-employee-policy -lead-to-customer-loyalty-costco-and-hp-prove-it-can.

[9] "Net Promoter Benchmarking," SatMetrix Net Promoter Community, accessed August 3, 2014, http://www.netpromoter.com /why-net-promoter/compare.

[10] Alan B. Goldberg and Bill Ritter, "Costco CEO Finds Pro-Worker Means Profitability," *ABC News*, August 2, 2006, http://abcnews.go .com/2020/Business/story?id=1362779.

[11] John Warrilow, "One Question Can Predict the Future of Your Company," *Inc.*, June 24, 2011, http://www.inc.com/articles/201106 /whats-your-net-promoter-score.html.

[12] Sales Executive Council, *World-Class Sales Coaching: Building A First-Line Manager Coaching Program*, 2007, https://sec.executive board.com/public/PosterPromo/SEC First-line Manager Coaching Program.pdf, 13–14.

CONCLUSION

[1] Dee Hock, *Birth of the Chaordic Age* (San Francisco: Berrett-Koehler Publishers, 1999).

[2] "Scientific Fish Story," *The New York Times*, August 25, 1901, http://query.nytimes.com/mem/archive-free/pdf?res=F60811F83F5B11738 DDDAC0A94D0405B818CF1D3.

[3] Rosabeth Moss Kantner, "The Enduring Skills of Change Leaders," in *Leader to Leader 2: Enduring Insights on Leadership,* ed. Frances Hesselbein and Alan Shrader (San Francisco: Jossey Bass, 2008).

ACKNOWLEDGMENTS

HEARTFELT THANKS TO OUR EXTRAORDINARY clients and colleagues who work so diligently to enable greatness in people and organizations everywhere. We are honored by our association with you and the significant work you do.

Special thanks to Breck England, Annie Oswald, and Sam Bracken for your tireless work on this project. None of this would be possible without the strategic and maniacal focus of our Franklin-Covey Practice Leaders—we are grateful to Kory Kogon, Gary Judd, Stephen M.R. Covey, Chris McChesney, Randy Illig, Sandy Rogers, and Catherine Nelson. And to Glenn, Debbie, and the entire team at BenBella Books for your synergistic partnership.

About the Authors

SHAWN D. MOON is an Executive Vice President of FranklinCovey, where he is responsible for the company's US and International direct offices, the Sales Performance Practice, and the Execution and Speed of Trust practices. Additionally, he oversees FranklinCovey's Government Business, Facilitator Initiatives, and Public Programs. Shawn has more than twenty-five years of experience in leadership and management, sales and marketing, program development, and consulting services.

Shawn was previously a principal with Mellon Financial Corporation, where he was responsible for business development for the company's Human Resources outsourcing services. Shawn coordinated activities within the consulting and advisory community for Mellon Human Resources and Investor Solutions.

Shawn received a bachelor of arts degree in English literature from Brigham Young University. Shawn and his wife, Michele, live in Lindon, Utah. They have four children. They enjoy music, theater, sporting activities, and the great outdoors.

SUE DATHE-DOUGLASS serves as Global Vice President of Leadership, Sales, and Delivery Effectiveness at FranklinCovey. Drawing on thirty-plus years of organizational and leadership experience, she is a catalyst for high performance and engagement at all levels of the organization.

Sue joined FranklinCovey in 1996 as a Leadership Delivery Consultant responsible for designing, developing, and delivering customized leadership engagement solutions that met the unique needs of her many clients.

Prior to joining FranklinCovey, Sue spent twenty-four years with the McDonald's Corporation as an internal organizational design and development consultant. She was responsible for strategic planning, operational integration, and quality management in the Atlanta region. She was also instrumental in helping McDonald's with its ongoing cultural, quality, and organizational transformation efforts.

Based in Scottsdale, Arizona, Sue spends more than 70 percent of the year traveling and working with leaders in more than one hundred countries. When not working, she enjoys walking, hiking, reading, and every minute she spends with her husband and two dogs.

About FranklinCovey

FRANKLINCOVEY CO. (NYSE:FC) IS A global company specializing in performance improvement. We help organizations achieve results that require a change in human behavior. Our expertise is in seven areas: leadership, execution, productivity, trust, sales performance, customer loyalty, and education. FranklinCovey clients have included 90 percent of the Fortune 100, more than 75 percent of the Fortune 500, thousands of small- and mid-sized businesses, as well as numerous government entities and educational institutions. FranklinCovey has more than forty direct and licensee offices providing professional services in more than 140 countries. For more information, visit www.franklincovey.com.

THE ULTIMATE COMPETITIVE ADVANTAGE

FranklinCovey is a global company specializing in performance improvement. We help organizations achieve results that require a change in human behavior.

Our expertise is in seven areas:

LEADERSHIP

Develops highly effective leaders who engage others to achieve results.

EXECUTION

Enables organizations to execute strategies that require a change in human behavior.

PRODUCTIVITY

Equips people to make high-value choices and execute with excellence in the midst of competing priorities.

TRUST

Builds a high-trust culture of collaboration and engagement, resulting in greater speed and lower costs.

SALES PERFORMANCE

Transforms the buyer-seller relationship by helping clients succeed.

CUSTOMER LOYALTY

Drives faster growth and improves frontline performance with accurate customer- and employee-loyalty data.

EDUCATION

Helps schools transform their performance by unleashing the greatness in every educator and student.

LEARN MORE

Want to learn more about how to dramatically improve the effectiveness of not just individuals, but your organization? Visit **www.franklincovey.com/uca**.

INDEX